quick**crafts**

30 fast and fun projects

LIVIA McREE

First published in the
United States of America by
Rockport Publishers, Inc.
33 Commercial Street
Gloucester, Massachusetts 01930-5089
Telephone: (978) 282-9590
Facsimile: (978) 283-2742
www.rockpub.com

ISBN 1-56496-840-5

10 9 8 7 6 5 4 3 2 1

Cover and Book Design: Leeann Leftwich
Production Design: Nancy Kowal
Cover Image: Photographs by Brian Piper
Photography, West Chester, Pennsylvania

Printed in China.

quick crafts

30 fast and fun projects

LIVIA McREE

GLOUCESTER MASSACHUSETTS

ROCKPORT PUBLISHERS

contents

6   Introduction

8   Know-How

14   30-MINUTE CRAFTS

16   Finial-Topped Bath Jars

18   Silver & Copper Beaded Napkin Rings

20   Suspended Veneer Frames

22   Layered Window Cards

24   Memory-Wire Bracelets

26   Stenciled Glass Bottles

28   Flower Appliqué Peg Rack

30   Etched Glass Candle Holder

32   Frosted Incense Bottle

34   Recycled-Linens Table Runner

36   TWO-HOUR CRAFTS

38   Gilded Bud Vases

40   Laced Letter Holder

42   Embossed Paper Bowl & Tray

44   Cut-Paper Window Shade

46   Collaged & Stamped Display Shelf

48   Upholstery-Tack Shelf

50   Hand-Illustrated Cocktail Napkins

52   Crumpled-Copper Candle Shades

54   Vintage-Paper Keepsake Boxes

56   Etched Ceramic Mug & Saucer

58 AFTERNOON CRAFTS

60 Flowerpot Trellis

62 Quilt-Inspired Felt Coasters

64 Braided-Rag Trivet

66 Metalwork Appliqué Frame

68 Craft-Time Clock

70 WEEKEND CRAFTS

72 Beaded Paper Valance

74 Easy Embroidered Bed Linens

76 Checkerboard Iron-on Veneer Tray

78 Pocketed Picnic Cloth

80 No-Sew Handbag

82 A GALLERY OF QUICK CRAFTS

95 PATTERNS

104 RESOURCES

107 ABOUT THE AUTHOR

108 ACKNOWLEDGMENTS

introduction

This book is intended to be a helpful guide and inspiring reference for both the casual and the constant crafter. Hopefully, the casual crafter will be encouraged to experiment with new materials and techniques, and the constant crafter will discover new tricks, tips, and ideas that make the process more enjoyable and productive. With so many things to do and so little time to do them, it's often the recreational activities, such as crafting, that get put off. But crafting is one of the most rewarding ways to spend time—it can be both relaxing and invigorating, expressive, therapeutic, and best of all, tangible.

Regardless of a hectic family life, long work hours, or a lack of confidence, productive crafting time can be squeezed in here and there with a minimum of effort. Even during the holiday season, making gorgeous, impressive gifts doesn't have to be overwhelming. Don't worry about skill level either; anyone with the desire to do so can make any project in this book. And never be afraid to make mistakes or "color outside the lines." Mistakes often lead to great discoveries.

With this in mind, the projects in this book were designed to be made within a specific amount of time: thirty minutes, two hours, an afternoon, and a weekend. Tips and shortcuts are sprinkled throughout the pages to help make the projects even quicker. And on the following few pages, there is handy information that should be read before starting projects, regarding tools and techniques that will help streamline the crafting process.

Ideally, crafts are both beautiful and practical. I hope that every handmade item inspired by this book finds its way into an appreciative home, to be used and enjoyed in everyday life.

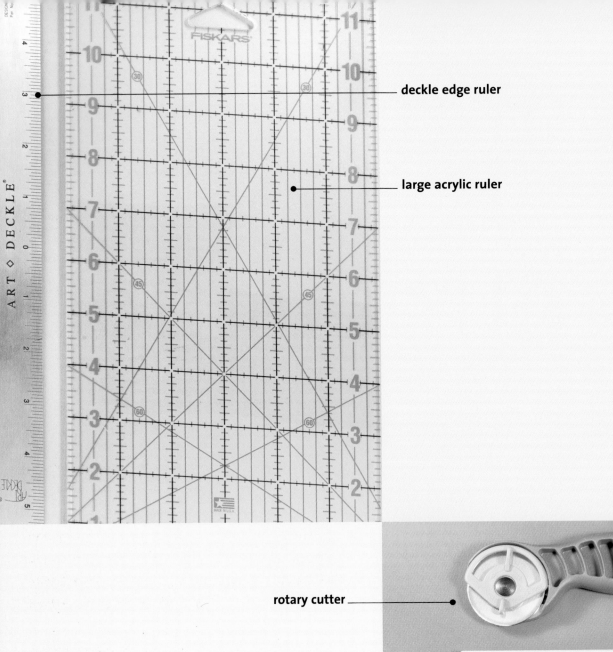

deckle edge ruler

large acrylic ruler

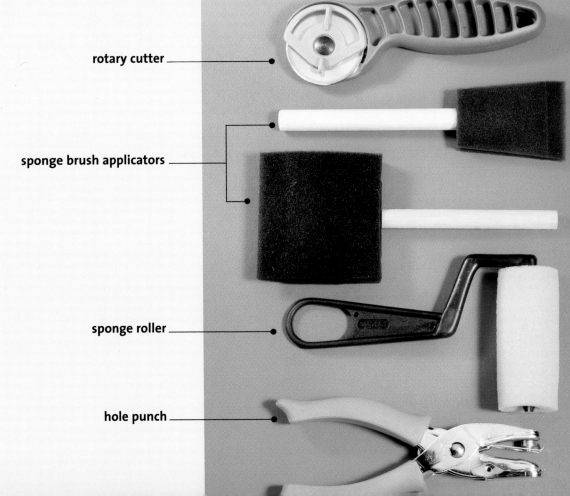

rotary cutter

sponge brush applicators

sponge roller

hole punch

know-how

BASIC TOOLS

• The right tool can make a project so much easier. And when time is limited, the right tools are essential. Start with the basics—**pencils**, **erasers**, **scissors**, and **masking tape**. Then get these useful items that will streamline crafting:

• Use a **rotary cutter**, **clear ruler**, and **cutting mat with grid** to measure and cut paper, fabric, veneer, and even metal in one easy step. Both the ruler and mat have guidelines and measurements on them that help keep cuts straight and squared up with a minimum of effort. Use a **deckle-edge ruler** with centering measurements to decoratively and quickly tear paper.

• Use a **craft knife** instead of scissors when intricate cutting is needed. The blades are removable, and there are many different shapes, sizes, and styles available for a variety of purposes.

• **Hole punches** add a quick embellishment to paper and embossing metal.

• **Round-nose pliers** and **wire cutters** are essential for wire crafting. Use the pliers to make smooth curls and loops with ease.

• **Spray adhesive** can be used on just about any surface for a nonstaining, smooth, even layer of glue. It also dries fast and is repositionable.

• Permanent, **quick-grab glue** is absolutely essential. There's nothing worse than waiting for glue to dry or watching things slip and slide because the glue hasn't firmed up yet. Buy craft formulas, not the ones from the hardware store, which tend to be more toxic and may damage fabric or delicate materials. Quick-grab glues are usually formulated for a variety of surfaces and can be used on almost anything, from paper to lace.

• **Washable fabric marking pens** are very handy for transferring patterns to fabric. Disappearing ink pens are also available, and the marks generally fade after a day or two. Always test the pens on a scrap first to be sure they don't stain.

• **Adhesive vinyl** is the best material for making stencils and patterns for etching and painting. It peels off nearly any surface without damaging it.

• **Sponge brush applicators** are the best painting tool. Use them for quick, even coverage. **Sponge rollers** can be used for larger surfaces.

• **Graph paper** and **tracing paper** are very useful for making patterns. Use graph paper to sketch out properly scaled, symmetrical patterns without having to make calculations or to laboriously double-check measurements. Use tracing paper to easily copy designs and motifs or to see how something will look on a surface

QUICK TECHNIQUES: PAPER

Cutting, Tearing, and Scoring Paper

Handmade and specialty papers often come in large sheets. It's helpful to use a sharp craft knife, a clear acrylic ruler, and a selfhealing cutting mat to trim large sheets of paper precisely and quickly, rather than marking and cutting the paper with scissors. For a decorative edge, use a rotary cutter or paper edging scissors. Wave, pinking, and deckle patterns are just a few of the available styles. For beautiful, organic-looking handmade papers, tearing provides a pleasing, soft edge, which often works better than a crisply cut edge. Simply trap the paper under a ruler, then pull the loose end up and over the ruler to tear it. To score paper, mat board, or cardboard, use a dulled craft knife or just press very lightly with a sharp one so as not to cut all the way through.

USE THE RIGHT GLUE

When working with paper, it is important to use the right glue. Many glues will saturate paper, causing discoloration. For cards and smooth papers, use spray adhesive. The bond, while not very strong, is usually sufficient for most purposes. If a stronger bond is called for, or if using heavily textured, handmade paper, use collage glue. It dries fast and is formulated to minimize color bleed. For thin or delicate papers, try applying the glue to the surface to which you are gluing the paper rather than to the paper itself to further guard against discoloration and color bleed.

QUICK TECHNIQUES: GLASS

Clean, Wash, & Dry

This is an important step that should be done thoroughly. Lint, oil from hands, and other grime interfere with both glass etching and painting. Once the glass is washed, wear gloves when handling it further, to prevent getting any fingerprints on it. Always use a lint-free rag to wipe glass as well.

Etching Tips

When etching glass, keep in mind that the higher the quality of the glass, the better the etching finish will be. If completely etching an inexpensive or imperfect piece of glass, streaks and unevenness in the finish may be obvious. Instead, try a spot design, which won't show the imperfections to the same degree.

Adhesive vinyl is the best material for making an etching pattern. When applying it, make sure that it is smooth and bubble-free on the glass. Sometimes, a bit of the adhesive will smear on the glass; just use rubbing alcohol and a cotton swab to remove it. Be sure not to let the alcohol seep under the vinyl.

Always apply as even a layer of etching creme as possible, and make sure it is at least a $1/8$" (3 mm) thick. Use a sponge applicator for best results; it has a soft, wide surface that won't disturb the vinyl etching pattern. Also, be careful when rinsing off etching creme, because it can damage ceramic or marble sinks. Wear dish gloves as well, because the creme is caustic.

Remember, etching "creme" is reusable, so scrape as much of it as possible back into the container.

QUICK TECHNIQUES: WOOD

Sanding & Filling

Most unfinished wooden items will be in good condition, ready to paint or decorate. Sometimes it's necessary to sand a rough spot. It's worth the trouble to do so, because these spots often become more visible after they're painted or stained. Use fine sandpaper, which won't leave deep scratches in the wood.

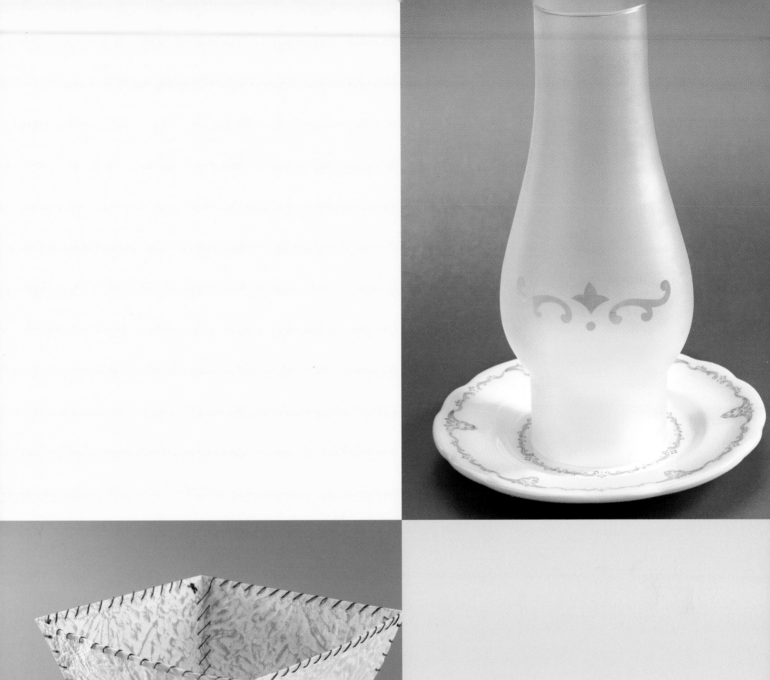
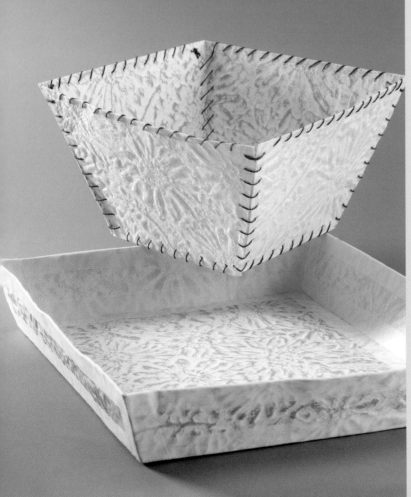

Items that have been nailed together will usually have a recessed area where they've been nailed. To fill the hole, use latex wood filler. The area can then be sanded and painted. The patch may be obvious

PROTECTIVE FINISHES

Apply a coat or two of sealer, varnish, or polyurethane to protect the wood, especially if it has been stained. Though it's not strictly necessary, it helps protect the surface and is a good idea if the object will be used often. Also, a high-gloss or matte finish can add an extra touch to the project.if the wood is stained, so try to make the stain gradually darker in that area to conceal it.

SHORTCUTS

Organize a Workspace

The biggest waste of time when crafting is trying to find materials and tools that seem to mysteriously disappear. Organizing a work area, even if it consists of only a box, is immeasurably helpful and time-saving. What tools and materials are used all the time? What supplies get used up most quickly? These are the things to have out and about. Everything else can be tucked away in storage boxes, but label them and keep them together in an area that isn't too difficult to access.

Ideally, a desk with a good light source and a nearby storage space is the best place to work. But, if this isn't possible, try organizing materials in see-through storage boxes, preferably wheeled ones. Then, wheel them out whenever and wherever they're needed, instead of spending time unpacking and transporting the necessary items one by one.

Choose a place to work with ample space to spread out, plenty of light, and a comfortable seat. This deceptively simple advice is crucial for a pleasant and efficient craft session. And, if organizing an area just for crafting, try to keep it uncluttered but packed with inspiring pictures, references, magazines, and books that are often flipped through for ideas.

GATHER MATERIALS FIRST

Before starting out, read through a project's directions. Some of the materials will have to be purchased. But before running out to a bunch of stores, figure out what can be substituted. A little digging around the house and some creative brainstorming can yield interesting new items to work with. Do not begin the project until all the materials are gathered to avoid having to get up and start looking for things. This can be very distracting as well as disruptive.

ASSEMBLY LINE CRAFTING

When making more than one of anything, use an assembly line approach to speed up the process. For example, if making cards, cut the paper for all the cards first, then fold them all, etc. Enlist friends and family to help, too. Divide the labor by assigning one step of the process to each person.

Get in the Zone—Be in the Mood

Since crafting is a creative process, it's important to feel like doing it. This feeling might not always coincide with free time. When this happens, try to get in the mood by reading a new craft magazine, looking at an art book, or even browsing the aisles of the local craft store. Be excited about doing the project—it will get done in no time.

thirty-minute crafts

Thirty minutes doesn't seem like enough time to do much of anything, especially make something by hand. But with a few simple materials and a specific plan of action, a half hour is all that's needed to create something new. Start with unadorned, simple materials. A plain glass jar, a wine bottle, a few pretty napkins—these are just a few of the materials used in this chapter as a canvas for creative expression.

The secret to creating a craft in no time is to bring together finished items in new ways, or to simply add a few key embellishments. The Etched Glass Candle Holder on page 30 simply consists of a china plate and a plain glass chimney. Etch on the chimney a design taken from the plate, and the two pieces come together to make something new—and in a snap. An even simpler project, the Recycled-Linens Table Runner on page 34, involves playing with the arrangement of beautiful linens to transform them into a table runner.

Quick Tips: Don't throw out the old or abused junk around the house, such as frames, glasses, or boxes. Instead, start thinking of ways to jazz them up with a minimum of effort. Beads, paint, or some other small, added detail may be all they need to give them a new life!

With the variety of finials available and the endless possibilities for finishing wood, this project is easy to customize to any decor. Make a matching set like the ones seen here, or use different finials in coordinating colors. Make sure the jars have smooth, flat-topped lids, and clean them thoroughly to remove any residue that might interfere with the bonding adhesive.

finial-topped bath jars

starting out:

Be sure to use a quick-grab, clear-drying adhesive that will bond glass to wood. Craft supply stores carry suitable adhesives that are generally less toxic than the industrial varieties found at hardware stores.

MATERIALS

- glass jars
- wooden finials
- quick-grab adhesive
- stain, paint, or other wood finish

1 **Decorate the finials.** Paint, stain, or gild the finials and let them dry. Blue wood stain and a metallic gilding paste in shades of blue were used here. Leave the bottom of the finials unfinished to ensure a strong bond between the wood and the glass.

2 **Bond the finials to the jars.** First, clean the tops of the jars thoroughly and let them dry. Squeeze a mound of adhesive on the bottom of the finial, concentrating it in the center. Attach the finials to the jars by applying firm, even pressure for about one minute. Don't worry about wiping away any adhesive that may have oozed out from under the finials. Let them dry completely, until the finials are firmly in place. Then, use a craft knife to cut away any excess adhesive from the base of the finials.

QUICK TIPS

Many finials come with screws in the base, but these can be easily pulled out with pliers.

To make sure your finial is centered on the jar lid, use a ruler to find the center of the lid, then mark it with a dot using a permanent marker.

 SHORTCUT/VARIATION:

Try using cork-topped jars and finished finials to create a set of kitchen containers. If the cork tops are large enough, simply screw the finials into place. If not, use any quick-grab adhesive or hot glue to attach the finials.

Few beads are used to make these napkin rings, so it's worth splurging on sterling silver and real copper. To make a standard napkin ring that is about 1 1/2"(4 cm) in diameter, plan a beaded design that is about 5" (13 cm) long. The rings seen here have five oval segments with five copper accent beads in between.

silver&
copper
beaded napkin rings

starting out:

Take four short strands of 20-gauge wire to the bead store to make sure that your beads of choice have holes large enough to accommodate the wire. The copper accent beads should be able to accommodate four strands of wire. The silver beads will only be threaded with wire once. Using a thinner wire will make the napkin ring too flimsy, and thicker wire will be difficult to manipulate.

1 **Cut two pieces of wire.** They should each be 9" (23 cm) long to make a napkin ring about 1 1/2" (4 cm) wide. Slip one accent bead over both pieces of wire and hold it 2" (5 cm) from the ends of the wires. Tape the wire ends down to hold the bead securely at this point.

2 **String beads on wire.** Next, slip a sequence of beads over each wire separately. Then slip another accent bead over both pieces of wire. Gently pull the beaded section apart to form an oval. Finish beading the napkin ring, keeping the beads tightly together.

3 **Close the ends.** After finishing the last beaded section, remove the tape from the other end. Bend the wire into a circle. Bring the wire ends from the last beaded section through the initial accent bead and pull both of them through. Pull both ends of the napkin ring in opposite directions until all the beads fit closely together. Then, tightly wrap the loose ends of the wires around the sides of the adjacent accent bead to hold the ring together. Clip the excess wire.

SHORTCUT/VARIATION:
Try stringing opaque, handmade glass beads on elastic cord. Make sure that there are no spaces between the beads when knotting the cord to close the napkin rings. Then push the knot into an adjacent bead. Use a toothpick if the bead holes are small.

MATERIALS

- silver and copper beads, assorted sizes and styles
- 20-gauge copper or silver wire
- wire cutters or old scissors
- masking tape

These custom-sized frames are perfect for a series of related photos or small items

such as pressed flowers, stamps, or drawings. Intricate cut patterns, like the corners

on these frames, can be produced effortlessly using paper-edging scissors, which cut

through veneer easily. Many effects are possible with the wide variety of decorative

edging scissors available.

suspended
veneer frames

starting out:

Determine the size of the frame based on the size of the image to be used. The frames seen here are 4" (10 cm) square, with a 1" (3 cm) border around the 2" (5 cm) square picture opening. Wood veneer can be found at craft supply and woodworking stores, often in assorted packs of 8 1/2" x 11" (22 cm x 28 cm) sheets. Avoid using oak veneer, which is very hard and can splinter when cut with paper edgers.

1 **Cut and punch the veneer.** Measure, mark, and use a craft knife to cut out two pieces of veneer in contrasting colors. Cut out the center opening as well. Next, use corner-edging scissors on one of the pieces of veneer to cut all four corners. Lay this trimmed piece on top of the second piece of veneer, and tape the two together. Punch holes in the top and bottom center of the frame. Repeat this procedure to make as many frames as desired. Then, remove the tape and lay all the veneer frames on a piece of newspaper and finish with a few quick, short bursts of spray sealer or varnish, if desired. Use the spray in a well-ventilated area or outdoors.

2 **Place the pictures in the frames.** If a protective cover is desired, cut out pieces of acetate 1/4" (6 mm) larger than the opening of the frames. Use a glue stick to adhere the acetate to the decorative-edged veneer. Position the image as desired, and secure with tape or other adhesive. Next, use quick-grab adhesive to glue the top and back frame pieces together.

3 **String the frames together.** Arrange the frames on a table spacing them out as desired for the finished project. Use this layout to roughly measure and cut a length of embroidery floss, string, or cord twice as long as the layout, plus 12" (30 cm) extra. Next, bring both ends of the string together, and then make a knot in the opposite end leaving a small loop for hanging. Slip a wooden bead up to the knot, then make another knot under it to keep it in place. Be sure to use beads larger than the holes punched in the veneer. Thread another bead on the string. Then, bring the string through the front of the top hole in the first frame, down the back of the frame, and out through the bottom hole; add another bead. Make knots in the string around each bead to keep them from slipping, making sure the string is taut against the back of the frame. Continue until each frame is attached.

SHORTCUT/VARIATION:
Make the frames double sided to create a photo mobile. Use two pieces of veneer for each frame, but adhere them back to back. Slip in images back to back as well. Instead of trimming the frame corners with corner edgers, trim each side of the frame with edging scissors for a decorative finish.

MATERIALS

- wood veneer in contrasting colors
- acetate (optional)
- pictures of choice
- embroidery floss or string
- wooden beads
- quick-grab adhesive
- glue stick
- spray acrylic sealer or varnish
- masking tape
- decorative corner edging scissors
- 1/8" (3 mm) hole punch
- craft knife

QUICK TIPS

For added detail, position the grain of the wood intentionally when assembling the frames. In all the tops of the frames seen here, the grain is vertical, and in all the back pieces the grain is horizontal.

When selecting the beads, make sure a single knot is enough to prevent the beads from slipping. If not, try a thicker string or beads with smaller holes.

Use these easy-cut cards to frame fabric, beautiful paper, or a special photo. Chinese bookbinding cloth with a woven pagoda pattern was slipped behind a cutout of a simplified house shape to make the change-of-address card shown oposite bottom. Try using damaged, embroidered linens or other pretty fabric scraps to make unusual, mixed-media cards. For a special anniversary card, frame a sweet photo of the couple, as shown opposite right. Use calligraphy, a printer, or a rubber stamp for the greeting inside.

layered window cards

MATERIALS

- **large sheet of card stock or other smooth, heavy-weight paper**
- **assorted papers for layering**
- **collage glue**
- **spray adhesive**
- **sponge brush**
- **craft knife**
- **paper edgers (optional)**

starting out:

If making more than one card, cut out all the papers for them first. This assembly-line method will save time—and it makes it easier for other people to help.

1 **Cut the paper for the card.** Measure, cut, and mark a piece of card stock or other heavyweight paper into a 16 $\frac{1}{2}$" x 7" (42 cm x 18 cm) rectangle to make the card. Score the rectangle twice, to make three 5 $\frac{1}{2}$" x 7" (14 cm x 18 cm) sections. Fold it into a Z shape.

2 **Cut out the window.** Use the patterns on page 96, or, create your own, to make a stencil. Draw the pattern on the back of the card's front flap, then cut it out. Residual pattern lines won't need to be erased since they will not show; the first two sections of the card will be glued together to make the frame.

3 **Add the paper accents.** Select a background paper, and cut out a piece smaller than 5 $\frac{1}{2}$" x 7" (14 cm x 18 cm). Be sure it is large enough to back the entire cutout pattern. Use collage glue and a sponge brush to apply the paper and seal the card frame. Glue any desired accents to the card.

4 **Make the envelope.** Cut a 19" x 6 $\frac{1}{2}$" (48 cm x 17 cm) rectangle for the envelope. Score the rectangle to make two 8" x 6 $\frac{1}{2}$" (20 cm x 17 cm) sections and one 3" x 6 $\frac{1}{2}$" (8 cm x 17 cm) section, which will be the envelope flap. Fold the scorings toward each other to make the envelope. Use a thin smear of collage glue along the side edges to seal it, about 1/4" (6 mm) wide (but no wider). Cut the envelope flap with paper edgers or add a strip of matching paper to coordinate it with the card. For a closure, use a small piece of paper and spray adhesive.

SHORTCUTS/VARIATIONS:
Cut a simple square for the card window, then slip in duplicate photographs or pictures to make mass quantities of a card for the holidays or a party. Choose a patterned or lightly textured paper for the card to make it more interesting.

Memory wire can be used to make jewelry without worrying about closures or complicated stringing techniques. The wire expands to easily fit wrists, necks, and ankles while retaining its shape perfectly without being constricting. The beads used for these bracelets are made of handmade glass and are sold in an assorted package of coordinating colors. This makes it fast and easy to design a piece of jewelry, and there are bound to be a few inspiring and unusual beads in the bunch.

memory- wire bracelets

MATERIALS
- handmade glass beads
- memory wire
- wire cutters
- round-nose pliers
- tape

starting out:

Choose beads that are no longer than $\frac{1}{2}$" (1 cm) because larger beads are very difficult to ease over the curved wire.

1 **Cut the wire.** Wrap a section of memory wire around the wrist (or neck or ankle), and add 1" (3 cm) to the length. Cut the wire at this point using wire cutters. Be careful when cutting memory wire. It is very springy and has a tendency to go flying.

2 **String the beads.** Select the beads for the bracelet. To plan the sequence of the beads, lay out the beads side by side on the sticky side of a piece of tape. The tape should be the same length as the wire plus $\frac{1}{2}$" (1 cm) on either end. Next, wrap a piece of tape on the wire $\frac{1}{2}$" (1 cm) from one end to secure the beads. Then, string the beads.

3 **Close the ends of the bracelet.** When the beads are all in place, use round-nose pliers to curl the end of the wire into a loop. Then, remove the tape on the other end and curl it into a loop as well. Make sure the beads are snug against each other.

 SHORTCUT/VARIATION:
For a more open look, use only a few special handmade beads. Hold them in place by wrapping thin wire around the bracelet or necklace close to the bead ends.

Glass painting is often tricky business. Drippy paint, uneven lines, and smearing are just a few of the problems that interfere with achieving a stained glass look. An easy way to control glass paint is to use custom stencils made with hand punches and adhesive vinyl, which minimizes paint seepage. Try bringing mismatched cups and glasses together into a set by painting the same design on all of them.

stenciled glass bottles

starting out:

Both heat-set and air-dry glass paints can be used for this project, but be sure to use heat-set paint for a durable finish if painting glassware that will need to be washed or handled often. Also, try acrylic enamel paints for an opaque, high-gloss finish.

MATERIALS

- glass bottle
- glass paint
- adhesive vinyl
- hand punch
- sponge brush
- soft round or flat brush

1 **Make the stencil.** Cut out squares of adhesive vinyl and punch out patterns in the centers. A frog-patterned punch is used here. Then place them around a clean, dry glass. The punch-outs can be used too, as shown with the cylindrical jar. Stick punch-outs around the glass in a row, then apply strips of adhesive vinyl on both sides of the row.

2 **Paint the glass.** Use a round or flat brush to paint inside the square stencils. Brush from the edges towards the center, pressing as lightly as possible. For the reverse-stencil stripes, use a sponge brush that is the same width of the stripes to paint a smooth, even line in one stroke. Carefully remove the vinyl before the paint is dry. Otherwise, it may peel up with the stencil.

QUICK TIPS

Press the vinyl firmly to the glass, making sure there are no air bubbles. Use a damp cotton swab to remove any paint seepage after removing the stencil.

Load the brush only half way with paint, so that it doesn't pool up inside the stencil.

3 **Heat-set the paint.** If necessary, heat-set the paint following the manufacturer's directions. Sometimes a twenty-four-hour drying period is called for to prevent the paint from bubbling as it is heated. To dry the paint quicker, place the glass in a cool oven and heat it for ten minutes at 150 degrees Fahrenheit [65 celsius]. Then, turn up the heat to the temperature called for by the manufacturer and continue to set. Let the glass cool completely before removing it from the oven.

 SHORTCUT/VARIATION:
Trying combining glass etching and painting. Add details to etched designs, such as flowers or leaves.

Wooden appliqués are a fast and easy way to add beautiful, carved details to simple, unfinished wooden items. There always seems to be a shortage of places to hang hats, coats, towels, bags—so why not make racks accented with appliqués for all those places where everyday things seem to pile up? Or, make a special rack for drying and displaying flowers and herbs.

wood *appliqué* peg rack

starting out:

Check the appliqués before applying them to make sure they rest flush against the peg rack. If they don't, gently rub them in a circular motion against fine sandpaper to flatten.

1 **Paint the peg rack.** First, sand any rough spots on the rack. Paint the pegs and the edges of the rack one color and the backboard of the rack another. Light shades of yellow and green were used here for an uplifting, springtime feel. Use fast-drying acrylic craft paints and a sponge brush for quick and easy application.

2 **Paint the appliqués.** Using a round or flat brush, paint the appliqués, and let them dry. Next, use a thin liner brush and a darker shade of paint to accentuate any carved details in the appliqués. The flowers seen here are painted light orange with medium orange accents.

3 **Apply the appliqués.** Determine where to place the appliqués, measuring if necessary and marking with a pencil. Squeeze a small dab of quick-grab adhesive on the center back of each appliqué, and firmly press them into place. Finish the rack with a coat of spray sealer or varnish, if desired.

 SHORTCUT/VARIATION:
Apply the appliqués first, then use spray paint to finish the whole rack in a solid color. Try metallic, enamel, or faux-finish spray paint.

MATERIALS
- peg rack
- wooden appliqués
- acrylic paints
- quick-grab adhesive
- spray acrylic sealer or varnish
- sponge brush
- liner brush
- round or flat brush
- fine sandpaper

QUICK TIP

Use masking tape to ensure a straight, painted line. First, paint the edges yellow, and allow to dry. Apply masking tape over the yellow areas just to the edge of the backboard, and then paint the backboard green. Always paint the lighter color first, in this case yellow, because it won't show through the darker color.

Glass chimneys can be found at home centers and hardware stores in a variety of shapes and sizes. Pair one with an orphaned or antique china plate for an old-fashioned, beautiful candle holder. To create a matched set, focus on one simple element in the plate's design and draw or trace it to make a motif that can be etched on the shade.

etched glass
candle holder

starting out:

Be sure to apply a thick, uniform layer of etching creme for an evenly frosted shade. Be careful not to let any creme linger inside the shade when rinsing off the excess, or a faint etching will be visible on the outside.

1 **Create a motif for the chimney.** Determine the size of the motif to be etched by cutting out a piece of graph paper and holding it to the shade. Draw a simple motif on graph paper, using the paper's lines as a guide to create a symmetrical design. If using the china plate as inspiration, try tracing a design from the plate first. Then sketch a larger version on the graph paper. Next, cut the pattern out of the paper and trace it on a piece of adhesive vinyl using a permanent marker. Use a craft knife to cut the pattern out of the vinyl, making sure not to cut into the pattern.

2 **Etch the chimney.** Wash and dry the chimney with a lint-free rag. Firmly press the vinyl pattern to the chimney. Following the manufacturer's directions, apply a thick even layer of creme to the glass with a sponge applicator. Wait five minutes, then use the applicator to scrape off as much of the creme as possible and put it back in the bottle. Rinse off the remaining creme under warm, running water, and remove the vinyl pattern. Be sure to wear rubber gloves when working with etching creme.

 SHORTCUT/VARIATION:
Use a large hour-glass-shaped hurricane shade and a bright, solid-colored plate to make a striking summertime centerpiece for an outdoor gathering. Etch a bold, easy-to-cut design on the plate and the shade, such as stripes.

MATERIALS

- glass chimney
- china dessert plate or saucer
- graph paper
- adhesive vinyl
- etchall™ glass etching creme
- sponge brush applicator
- craft knife
- rubber gloves

QUICK TIP

Since the sketched motif needs to be cut out of adhesive vinyl, keep the lines very simple.

Use any bottle that doesn't have a screw top to make this dreamy incense holder. To use, fit an incense stick with a wooden end into an ordinary key ring; the wooden end will keep the ring in place. Make sure the stick hangs straight down the middle of the bottle by centering it within the key ring, then relax and watch the bottle fill with thin ribbons of smoke!

frosted incense bottle

MATERIALS

- **glass bottle**
- **key ring**
- **precut glass etching stencils**
- **etchall™ glass etching creme**
- **sponge brush applicator**
- **adhesive vinyl**
- **craft knife**
- **rubber gloves**

starting out:

There are a wide variety of precut stencils especially made for etching glass. Mix and match motifs to create unique, quick, and easy patterns.

1 **Apply the precut stencils.** Soak the labels off the bottle in hot water, then wash and dry the bottle with a lint-free rag. Try not to get any fingerprints on the areas of the glass to be etched. Apply the stencils to the bottle pressing firmly in place. Randomly placed stars of various shapes and sizes were used here.

2 **Etch the bottle.** Following the manufacturer's directions, apply a thick even layer of creme to the glass using a sponge applicator. Wait five minutes, then use the sponge applicator to scrape off as much of the creme as possible and put it back in the bottle. Rinse off the remaining creme under warm, running water and remove the stencils. Be sure to wear rubber gloves when working with etching creme.

 SHORTCUT/VARIATION:
Etch only one central motif on darkly colored glass, rather than reverse-etching an entire bottle. Cut a pattern from a square of vinyl and etch only within the square. Dark-colored glass will conceal the incense stick within the bottle as well as the etching.

This table runner was made using two napkins and a place mat from a matching set of Turkish table linens. Napkins are usually square while place mats are rectangular, and the height of a place mat will generally correspond to the height of a matching napkin. This makes it easy to create a table runner of consistent height. Since the place mat seen here has a beautiful, knotted fringe, it was joined to the napkins on its longer edges instead.

recycled-
linens table runner

starting out:

Play with the arrangement of the napkins and place mats before fusing them. Try using all napkins, all place mats, or a combination of both, like the runner seen here.

1 **Apply fusing tape.** Press the linens to remove any wrinkles or creases. Measure the shorter end of a napkin, and cut two pieces of fusing tape to that length. Following the manufacturer's directions, iron the fusing tape with the paper side up on one short edge of each napkin (front side). If necessary, first trim the tape to a narrower width to avoid covering parts of the napkins that should remain visible.

2 **Iron the place mat to the napkins.** Tape the napkins down on an ironing board to secure them. Align the edges of the place mat with the edges of the fused areas on the napkins, and iron the place mat to the napkins. Be sure to prevent the place mat from shifting while ironing.

 SHORTCUTS/VARIATIONS:
Try using mismatched napkins of the same size to make an interesting patchwork runner. Accent plain, white napkins using fabric paint and large foam stamps. Iron store-bought appliqués around a runner to create a unifying border, or fuse fringe to the ends of a runner.

MATERIALS
- 2 napkins
- 1 place mat
- paper-backed fusing tape
- masking tape
- iron

QUICK TIP
Lay a thin cloth over linens before ironing to avoid damaging fine or delicate material.

two-hour crafts

Everything in this section is designed to take two hours or less to create, which is enough time to make more than you might think! From vases to window shades, these crafts are perfect for gift giving and home decoration. Even if two hours seems impossible to set aside, don't despair. Most of these projects can be easily divided into a couple of one-hour sessions or four half-hour sessions.

One important thing to remember when crafting on a tight schedule is to assemble materials before beginning the project. Lots of stopping and starting can be distracting and counterproductive. It also helps to keep supplies in one place, so there's no need to waste time searching for a craft knife or that special piece of paper.

Quick Tips: While most of the crafts in this book use easy-to-find, everyday materials, some days there just isn't enough time to go shopping for even the most ordinary supplies. When this happens, try to change the project to fit the materials on hand. Use a piece of wrapping paper instead of handmade paper, a utility knife instead of a craft knife, an old glass cup instead of a real vase. This is sure to lead to great discoveries, shortcuts, and unique projects.

The secret to quick, perfect gilding is to use spray adhesive and forget the size. Size, a glue traditionally used with metal leaf, takes a long time to dry and sometimes needs to be applied twice. Repositionable spray adhesive, available at any art or craft supply store, dries in a few minutes in a smooth, even coat—making brush strokes a thing of the past.

gilded bud vases

starting out:

Variegated metal leaf is heat-treated to create colorful patterns ranging from pink to blue. Different brands have different patterns, such as the stripes and sunbursts used here. Plan the project with this in mind, and select a vase with a complementary shape.

1 **Apply the adhesive.** Clean and wash vases. In a well-ventilated or outdoor area, spray a coat of adhesive on the vases. Be sure to protect the surrounding surfaces from the adhesive with paper, or spray the vases in a cardboard box. Test the glue first on a piece of paper to be sure the nozzle isn't clogged, because this will cause bumps on the surface of the vase. One quick, even coat is all that's needed. Wait a few minutes until the glue sets.

2 **Gild the vase.** Carefully tear the variegated patterns from the leaf and apply them first. For example, if using stripes, apply them first to be sure they line up, then fill in the rest of the vase with the solidly colored parts of the leaf. For a bud vase, two or three 5 $\frac{1}{2}$" x 5 $\frac{1}{2}$" (14 cm x 14 cm) sheets should be sufficient.

3 **Apply gloss varnish or enamel.** Using a soft brush, apply a minimum of two coats following the manufacturer's directions. If using a water-based product, be careful when filling the vase with water and wipe away drips quickly to protect the finish.

SHORTCUT/VARIATION:
Instead of gilding the entire vase, create gilded shapes such as triangles, squares, or intricate hand-punched designs using adhesive vinyl. Center the cutout within a large piece of adhesive vinyl, then apply the vinyl to the vase. Make sure the rest of the vase is protected from the spray adhesive. Complete the gilding and varnishing before removing the vinyl, but remove the vinyl before the varnish is dry to prevent peeling.

MATERIALS
- glass vase
- variegated metal leaf
- spray adhesive
- soft brush
- gloss varnish or enamel

QUICK TIP
Leaf is very delicate, but don't be afraid to handle it or let it wrinkle when applying it. Just rub it gently into place with your fingers, then use a soft brush to whisk away the excess.

This handy letter holder is a great way to organize incoming and outgoing mail. One lightweight but sturdy piece of mat board is scored and folded, then covered with handmade paper. With the wide variety of paper colors and textures available, it is easy to customize this project to match any room. Lacing together the front and back helps keep letters in place, strengthens the structure, and provides an easy way to personalize the holder. Try using ribbon, elastic cord, or wire instead of string, and experiment with different lacing patterns.

laced
letter holder

starting out:

MATERIALS

- mat board or cardboard
- handmade paper in yellow and natural or other assorted colors
- glue stick
- craft knife
- ¹/₈" (3 mm) hole punch (optional)
- string or twine

1 **Cut and score board.** Measure, mark, and cut out a 10" x 20" (25 cm x 51 cm) rectangle on a piece of mat board or sturdy cardboard. Beginning at one of the 10" (25 cm) ends, measure up 3 ³/₄" (9.5 cm) and 6 ³/₄" (17.5 cm) and mark lines straight across at both points. Score these lines with a craft knife and fold them to create a U-shape.

2 **Paper board.** Cut two 11" x 1" (28 cm x 3 cm) pieces of paper and use a glue stick to apply them to the underside of the scored joints. Make sure they wrap around to the front, and are tautly and smoothly adhered. This reinforces the joints and helps keep the holder's shape. Next, cut two 11" x 21" (28 cm x 53 cm) pieces of yellow paper. Apply the paper to the back and then the front of the holder. Fold the edges over each time and glue securely in place. Next, cut a 9 ¹/₂" x 6 ¹/₄" (24 cm x 16 cm) piece of natural-colored paper and apply it to the front of the mail holder, where it will be laced. Using the same paper, cut out and apply the envelope flap to the top of the holder.

3 **Lace board.** With an ¹/₈" (3 mm) hole punch, make holes ¹/₄" (6 mm) in all corners of the shorter front of the mail holder. Make corresponding holes on the back of the holder. The holes at top should be 6 ¹/₂" (17 cm) up from the bottom. Also make a hole at the top of the board for hanging. Cut 3 feet (.9 meter) of string and lace the front of the holder to the back. There are a number of different ways to do this. For the pattern seen here, see page 97. Knot the ends together at the back and secure with a dab of glue, or tie the ends in front with a bow. Also make a small knotted loop for hanging and thread it through the hole at the top of the holder.

4 **Add words and seal.** To spell MAIL, use rubber stamps, an alphabet stencil and paint, or handwriting. Cut out and layer two small, red circles of paper, one slightly larger than the other, to make the seal, or use a sticker, rubber stamp, or real wax.

 SHORTCUT/VARIATION:
Cut out one flat piece of board and cover with a piece of fabric 2" (5 cm) larger all around. Apply the fabric to the board using spray adhesive. Fold the edges to the back and secure with quick-grab, permanent fabric glue. Create a pocket with a prehemmed piece of fabric, such as a napkin or bandana. Glue the fabric around the board to create the pocket. Glue a ribbon loop to the back of the board for hanging.

This sturdy bowl and tray are made using heavyweight, handmade paper. For added strength as well as beauty, two pieces of paper are joined back to back to make each side. The pattern for this project can be adjusted to make bowls and trays of various sizes, so try making a set of matching containers to organize a desk. Be sure to choose a thick paper that is difficult to tear or roll.

embossed
paper bowl & tray

starting out:

Make a shorter bowl or taller tray by using a ruler to extend or shorten the lines of the side patterns. Just be sure to leave the base the same.

1 **Prepare the paper for cutting.** Spread out some newspaper in a well-ventilated or outdoor area, then use a heavy coat of spray adhesive to adhere two pieces of embossed paper in different colors back to back. Press the papers firmly together. Then, lightly spray the front and back with varnish or sealer. Let each side dry completely before proceeding.

2 **Mark and cut paper.** Enlarge or reduce the pattern on page 97 to the desired size, first making sure that your paper of choice will be large enough to accommodate it. Next, trace the pattern on the paper and cut out the pieces; one bottom and four sides for each container. For the bottom, cut out a square with each side the same length as the bottom edge of the container's side. For the bowl, punch holes along the edges as indicated on the pattern, if desired. The holes can also be made with the needle while lacing the bowl. Or the base and sides can be joined with linen tape like the tray seen here.

3 **Assemble the tray and bowl.** Use linen tape to assemble the tray. Cut a piece of tape slightly longer than the edge to be joined, then trim the excess tape after applying it. Begin by taping the bottom edge of each side to the base, then tape the side corners together. Apply tape to both the inside and the outside of each joined area. To lace the bowl together, thread an arm's length of string through a large needle and begin lacing the sides of the bowl to the bottom. Use an overhand stitch. Start a new piece of string for each side and tie them off inside the bowl.

SHORTCUT/VARIATION:
Embossed paper can often be found in plain white or off-white sheets. Try using a sponge brush with very little paint worked into it to highlight the embossed areas. Hold the brush nearly parallel to the paper while painting to avoid catching the recessed areas.

MATERIALS
• large, full-sized embossed paper sheets in two colors
• string, cord, or twine
• spray adhesive
• spray acrylic sealer or varnish
• linen tape
• 1/8" (3mm) hole punch
• needle with a large eye
• craft knife or scissors

This shade is prefect for a small, sunny window. The subtle effect of birds in flight is achieved by cutting out shapes from a piece of paper, then applying another sheet on top of it. Use a white or light-colored paper for the back sheet, and a darker color for the front. When selecting papers for this project, hold them up to the light to check for translucency. A color-blended yellow to blue unryu rice paper is used here for the front. White unryu rice paper is used for the back.

cut-paper
window shade

starting out:

If a full-sized sheet of paper is too small to fit the window, add additional strips of paper to make a larger shade. Since the joined edges will be visible when light shines through the shade, try cutting the edges in a pattern to add another element to the design. Try a miniaturized version first to see how it will look.

1 **Cut the pattern out of the paper.** Cut out the bird patterns on page 98, and trace them on the paper designated for the back of the shade. The birds seen here are arranged from bottom left to top right, getting smaller towards the top to suggest distance. Cut the birds out with a craft knife.

2 **Assemble the shade.** Lay the papers face down on newspaper and spray with adhesive. Use the spray in a well-ventilated area or outdoors. Cut a small piece of string and position it at the bottom center of one of the papers, to form a loop for hanging. Do not make a knot in the string, but press it firmly in place. Then apply the papers back to back. Use a blunt edge, such as the edge of a ruler, to gently burnish them together.

3 **Attach a stick or dowel for hanging.** Use a thin line of quick-grab adhesive to attach a bamboo stick or dowel to the top of the shade. Mount the stick on suction cups, hooks, or small nails. Use a small nail just above the middle of the stick to hang the shade open using the loop at the bottom, as shown in the photo to the right.

SHORTCUT/VARIATION:
For a quicker shade, use a hand punch along the edges of the paper. Try punching the front sheet rather than the back or alternating the punches on the front and back sheets.

MATERIALS

- tear-resistant, translucent paper, such as unryu rice paper
- stick or dowel
- quick-grab adhesive
- spray adhesive
- embroidery floss, string, or ribbon
- craft knife

This small shelf is perfect for displaying a cherished memento. Pieces of tissue paper

were collaged randomly over the shelf to give it a variegated patina reminiscent

of the mottled patterns in marble. The star stamping on the backboard serves as a

frame, drawing the eye toward the displayed object. Light and true blue inks were

layered using a simple stamp to build up the subtle but distinct pattern.

collaged &
stamped
display shelf

starting out:

Select paint, ink, and tissue paper in shades of the same color. This creates an interesting design that will show off whatever is on display, without detracting from it.

1 **Paint the shelf.** Sand the wood, if necessary, and remove all dust with a damp rag. With a foam brush, paint the shelf. Since the tissue paper becomes translucent when collaged, choose a light paint so that the color of the tissue isn't obscured. Light blue paint is used here.

2 **Collage the tissue paper on the shelf.** Tear bits of tissue, and apply them to the shelf and backboard using collage glue and a foam brush. Cover completely. When dry, apply a thin layer of glue over the tissue, and lay a whole sheet of tissue over the backboard. Wrap the edges around to the back and smooth the tissue down. Repeat the procedure for the shelf.

3 **Stamp a design on the tissue.** Stamp a border design around the edges of the backboard, using the different blues to build up the pattern. Work in towards the center. When the ink has dried, finish the shelf with a coat of spray sealer or varnish.

SHORTCUTS/ VARIATIONS:
Try layering different colors of tissue, which will blend to create new hues. Stamp just one central design on the backboard. Experiment with different colored inks and different stamps to build up a colorful abstract pattern.

MATERIALS

- small, unfinished wood shelf with backboard
- tissue paper
- acrylic paint
- stamp ink pads in two shades
- collage glue
- spray acrylic sealer or varnish
- sponge brush
- star stamp
- fine sandpaper

QUICK TIP

If you can't find a shelf with a backboard, add one to an existing shelf using a piece of scrap lumber and small nails.

The comforting, quiet environment of a classic, old library inspired

this project. Reminiscent of an upholstered chair, this shelf is the per-

fect home for a few cherished books. Use matching tacks to tie the shelf

to other furniture in a room, or use paint colors that will blend easily

into the environment.

upholstery-
tack shelf

starting out:

To plan the arrangement of the tacks, try cutting out a piece of corrugated cardboard the size of the edge or area where the tacks will be placed. Play with different sequences by simply sticking the tacks and pins in the cardboard. Then, tape the cardboard strips to the shelf and poke a pencil through the holes to transfer the pattern.

MATERIALS
- unfinished wooden shelf
- upholstery tacks
- escutcheon pins
- terra-cotta and nutmeg acrylic paints
- acrylic varnish
- spray acrylic sealer
- sponge brush
- hammer
- fine sandpaper
- terry cloth rag

1 **Apply a base coat.** First, sand any rough spots on the rack. Paint the shelf with two different shades of brown using a sponge brush. The shelf here was painted with a warm terra-cotta color. The edges with the tacks and pins were painted a dark, rich nutmeg color.

2 **Faux-finish the shelf.** In a disposable plastic container, mix one part of the darker paint, in this case nutmeg, with two parts of liquid acrylic varnish, to make 1 cup of the mixture. Stir well with a stick, then apply the varnish mixture to the shelf in dabs using a terry cloth rag. Concentrate the color around the edges of each surface and work towards the center, leaving the very middle fairly light. Smooth the varnish out using a dabbing rather than a wiping motion using the same cloth. When the finish is dry, spray the shelf with sealer.

QUICK TIP

Be sure to hit the tacks straight on when driving them in, because they may be diffi- cult to remove without damag- ing the wood.

3 **Nail in the tacks and pins.** Plan the pattern of the tacks and pins, then mark pencil dots on the shelf as a guideline. On the shelf here, the tacks and pins were evenly spaced in a simple alter- nating pattern along the edge, and evenly spaced pins were used to delineate the edges of the brackets. Nail in tacks and pins with a hammer.

SHORTCUTS/VARIATIONS:
Search the hardware store for decorative or interesting fasteners such as copper tacks or hand- cut nails. Also, try affixing a scrap of home decorating fabric over the top of the shelf using quick-grab glue. Finish with upholstery tacks.

The hand-illustrated designs on these napkins are easy to replicate, and it should only take a couple of hours to make a set of four. The secret to this seemingly labor-intensive project is to use a solid design that can be easily outlined and then quickly filled in with color. Once the repeating pattern is drawn two or three times, it becomes much quicker and easier to complete the rest.

hand-illustrated
cocktail napkins

starting out:

Linen napkins will most likely be transparent enough to easily trace a solid black pattern. If not, use a light box, or tape the napkins to a sunny window. Just outline the pattern first, then take the napkin down and fill in the design.

MATERIALS
- hemstitched cocktail napkins
- fine-tipped permanent fabric markers
- masking tape

1 **Prepare the pattern.** Photocopy the pattern on page 98 to fit within the borders of the napkin. Try several different sizes to see what works best. Wash and press the napkins to remove any wrinkles or creases, if necessary.

2 **Illustrate the napkins.** Tape the pattern to a work surface, then tape a napkin over it. Use a fine-tipped fabric marker to trace the pattern. Fill in the dotted border around the hemstitching by starting in the middle of each side and working out to the edges to help keep the dots evenly spaced.

 SHORTCUTS/VARIATIONS:
Try filling in a single design in the center of the napkins. Look at clip-art books or henna patterns for inspiration see Resources, page 104. For even quicker napkins, use a combination of wide- and fine-tipped markers to make simple stripes of varying widths, and color along the border or in the center of the napkins.

QUICK TIP

New markers may bleed more than desired. Test them on a piece of scrap linen first. To minimize any bleeding, practice using short, quick strokes to fill in the pattern, and don't let the tip of the marker linger on the fabric.

These cutout shades sparkle when lit, and they make the most out of candlelight. Crumpling soft embossing copper gives it added strength and durability, and it also creates more surface area to reflect light. Try leaving the shades outside for a real verdigris patina. For a dappled rainbow effect, hold the copper with a glove-protected hand over an open flame.

crumpled-
copper
candle shades

Use old scissors to cut metal, which is very dulling and can ruin a good pair of scissors. Also, change the craft knife blade often while cutting out the pattern. Save the discarded blades for other uses, such as scoring or cutting cardboard.

MATERIALS

- soft embossing copper
- fine copper wire mesh
- quick-grab adhesive
- old scissors
- hole punches
- craft knife
- fine-tipped permanent marker
- masking tape

1 **Cut out the patterns from the copper.** First, determine how large the shade should be by wrapping a rectangle of paper around the candle. Be sure there is at least 1/2" (1 cm) of clearance on all sides of the candle. There should also be 1/2" (1 cm) overlap on both short ends to close the shade. Add 1" (3 cm) to the height of the rectangle so that the top and bottom edges can be neatly folded over. Next, measure and cut the copper sheets using the paper pattern and a pair of old scissors. Then, use the sun pattern on page 99 to make a stencil. Tape down the copper, and transfer the image using a fine-tipped permanent marker. Cut out along the lines using a sharp craft knife.

QUICK TIPS

To make identically sized triangles, make a cardboard triangle and trace it randomly over the copper.

Metal shades may become hot if the candle has been burning for a while, so be careful when handling them.

2 **Crumple the copper.** Gently crumple the copper, being careful not to rip the delicate areas of the sun pattern. Then, smooth the metal back out. Use a rolling pin to flatten it out.

3 **Add the wire-mesh backing.** Cut a piece of wire mesh that is 1" (3 cm) shorter and about 1/2" (1 cm) less wide than the shade. Place it over the crumpled copper, and fold the top and bottom edge of the copper over 1/2" (1 cm) to secure the mesh in place. Use the edge of a ruler for a straight, even fold. Use a rolling pin to flatten the crease. Next, punch a border along the top and bottom edges, taking into account that the short ends will overlap by 1/2" (1 cm). Star and crescent punches were used here.

4 **Close the shades.** Use a thin line of quick-grab glue to close the shades. Overlap the short ends at least 1/2" (1 cm) and press firmly along the seam for about one minute. Then, wipe away or gently rub off any excess glue.

 SHORTCUT/VARIATION:
Try making a pleated shade from wire mesh. Fold the top and bottom edges over for a clean finish, then use a ruler to make neat folds. Lace the edges shut with fine-gauge copper wire.

Old papers, such as book pages, sheet music, maps, receipts, or newspapers often have an appealing, aged look that can be easily replicated with a simple antiquing solution. Try using actual vintage papers too, especially those with interesting graphics on them. Choose papers according to the purpose for which the box will be used, or select papers with a favorite theme, such as recipe clippings, sheet music, state maps, or black-and-white photos.

vintage-paper
keepsake boxes

starting out:

Find old books, magazines, and newspapers from yard sales, second-hand stores, or in those old, dusty attic boxes that haven't been opened in years. For a mail-order supplier of vintage collage papers, see Resources on page 104.

1 **Paint the box.** Paint the edges and the inside of the box with a muted color. It isn't necessary to paint the entire outer area of the box.

2 **Collage the boxes.** Tear paper strips as needed using a ruler. First, trap the paper under the ruler. Then slowly tear along the edge by pulling the paper up and towards the ruler. Use a sponge brush and thinned white glue or collage glue to apply the strips. Apply the glue directly to the box. Let the boxes dry completely before proceeding to the next step.

3 **Prepare and apply the antiquing varnish.** In a disposable plastic container, pour about 1 tablespoon of varnish, and add two drops of dark brown paint. Mix thoroughly, then test the mixture on a piece of paper. Add more varnish or paint to make a lighter or darker antiquing solution. Brush the mixture on the boxes, then apply a second coat to specific areas, such as the edges, to simulate an aged appearance.

SHORTCUTS/VARIATIONS:
Paint the entire box, then collage a single interesting image on each side. Or, use large hand punches to make confetti shapes, then collage them randomly on the box or along the edges.

MATERIALS

- papier-mâché or unfinished wooden box
- book pages, maps, or sheet music for collage
- acrylic paints, including dark brown
- collage or thinned, white craft glue
- acrylic varnish
- sponge brush
- soft synthetic brush
- ruler

QUICK TIPS

Choose a box that has a lid that is easy to remove or, better yet, is too loose. Once the box is painted and varnished, it will fit perfectly, and the finish won't be scuffed by a tight-fitting top.

To thin white glue to a workable consistency, use only a few drops of water and mix thoroughly. Adjust the mix as needed. The glue shouldn't be runny nor dry too quickly.

Etching creme works on a variety of surfaces, including ceramic glazes. The combination of matte and shiny surfaces is especially eye-catching on a ceramic piece. This effect works best on solidly colored items or when used to accent a particular area of a pattern. For example, etch the area around a flower to make it pop, or etch only the handle on a heavily decorated cup.

etched
ceramic cup & saucer

starting out:

Choose medium-to dark-colored ceramics. On pale or white glazes, the etched pattern will be very subtle.

1 **Divide the cup into stripes.** Measure the circumference of the cup and divide it into equal segments. Make sure there are an odd number of segments for an alternating etched and nonetched stripe pattern. Wash and dry the cup and saucer. Next, cut strips of adhesive vinyl the width of the stripes and place one in every other space on the cup.

2 **Squeeze a resist gel pattern on the saucer.** Squeeze dots of resist gel along the rim of the saucer. Let the gel dry until translucent and firm. Drying time depends on the thickness of the dot, so hold the nib of the bottle close to the surface of the cup when squeezing. This will force it to spread out, rather than up.

3 **Etch the cup and saucer.** Following the manufacturer's directions, apply a thick even layer of creme to the glass using a sponge applicator. Wait fifteen minutes, then use the sponge applicator to gently scrape off as much of the creme as possible and put it back in the bottle. Rinse the remaining creme off under warm running water and remove the vinyl pattern and the resist gel. Be sure to wear rubber gloves when working with etching creme.

SHORTCUTS/VARIATIONS:
Practice drawing designs and letters with resist gel, and make a freeform design or spell out words. Also, try revitalizing a set of old dishes or pulling together mismatched ware with a simple, matching motif.

MATERIALS
- ceramic cup and saucer
- adhesive vinyl
- etchall™ resist gel
- etchall™ glass etching creme
- sponge brush
- applicator
- craft knife
- rubber gloves

afternoon crafts

An afternoon spent crafting is one of the greatest pleasures in life, whether it is spent baking a cake, whittling, or making a frame for a special, treasured picture. The projects in this chapter will take approximately three to five hours to complete. Some projects, such as the Flowerpot Trellis and the Metalwork Appliqué Frame will take an afternoon to make only because of the necessary drying time for paints and finishes.

If it isn't feasible to set aside three to five hours for a project, these afternoon crafts can also be modified so that they take less time. Try simplifying the designs and choosing fast-drying finishes to shave off some time. Or, break the projects up into sessions so that they can be completed over a couple of days rather than one sitting. Try to finish an entire step before stopping to make it a bit easier to continue the next day.

Quick Tip: Though it isn't always possible, try to set aside personal crafting time so that the whole family understands and respects the need to focus for a few hours. Treat the crafting experience as an important, vital part of life. That attitude and effort will certainly lead to beautiful, accomplished artwork.

This trellis is a cinch to make and can be easily adjusted to fit any size and style of pot or planter. Assortments of narrow wooden strips are usually available at craft and hobby stores. Select balsa wood, which is very soft, or basswood, which is a little harder. Both are easy to cut with an ordinary craft knife. For added detail, also try incorporating miniature dollhouse moldings into the trellis design.

flowerpot trellis

MATERIALS

- $\frac{1}{4}$" (6 mm) wide squared balsa or basswood strips
- white and gray acrylic craft paint
- crackle medium
- quick-grab adhesive
- spray acrylic sealer or varnish
- small round or liner brush
- craft knife or hobby saw
- fine sandpaper
- ruler
- grid cutting mat

starting out:

If the trellis will be used outdoors, tap small finishing nails into a few joined areas to strengthen it. This will ensure that it doesn't come apart in harsh weather.

1 **Cut the strips for the trellis.** Place one of the wooden sticks in the pot in which the trellis will be placed. Mark how far out of the pot it should rise. Twice the height of the pot works well. Next, measure the width of the pot base. This will be the maximum distance between the two central sticks that will secure the trellis in the pot. Photocopy the desired pattern on page 99 in several different sizes to see what works best, then use it as a guide for cutting the strips. Measure, mark, and cut all the strips, and lay them on the pattern. Gently sand any rough edges.

2 **Assemble the trellis.** Use small dabs of quick-grab adhesive to assemble the trellis. First, lay all the vertical strips on a grid cutting mat, using the lines to keep the sticks squared up and parallel to each other. Then, begin applying the horizontal strips, again using the mat's guidelines to keep the sticks perpendicular to the vertical strips.

3 **Create the crackle finish.** Paint the whole trellis white using a small sponge brush. Let the trellis dry. Following the manufacturer's instructions, use a small, round brush to apply the crackle medium. When the medium is translucent and tacky to the touch, paint the trellis gray using a small round or liner brush. The crackling will begin to appear almost immediately as the gray paint dries. Try not to go over the same area twice with the gray paint, because it will obscure the crackled effect. Finally, spray the trellis with sealer or varnish when completely dry.

SHORTCUTS/VARIATIONS:
Trellis patterns are limitless. Try gradually tapering the ends of the vertical strips to make a rounded pattern. Or, make a simple, tapered lattice.

Felt is the perfect material for making casual coasters that are durable, washable, and stain resistant. These coasters feature traditional, easy-to-cut quilt block patterns, which can be adjusted for a variety of effects by simply changing the colors of each piece. Try making several identical coasters, and glue them down in rows on a larger piece of felt to make a place mat or trivet. Most quilt blocks like the ones seen here are designed to create an overall pattern when viewed together.

quilt-inspired
felt coasters

MATERIALS

- felt, in various colors
- quick-grab washable fabric glue
- straight pins
- sharp scissors
- embroidery floss and needle (optional)

QUICK TIP
If making the crazy quilt pattern (see photo, opposite page, top left), try cross-stitching along the seams for a traditional look. Apply the block pieces with a single, central dab of glue to one layer of felt, stitch, then apply the final backing layer to conceal the stitches.

1 **Make the coaster bases.** Cut out two 4" x 4" (10 cm x 10 cm) felt squares and glue them together along the edges. This makes the base of one coaster. If finishing the edges with embroidery floss, apply glue 1/2" (1 cm) in from the edges, because it is difficult to sew through glue once it has dried.

2 **Assemble the quilt blocks.** Photocopy the desired pattern on pages 100-101 twice. Plan the colors for each piece of the coaster top by sketching them in with colored pencils, crayons, or markers. Next, number and cut out each piece. Keep the other photocopy whole, also colored and numbered, as a guide to refer to while assembling the coaster. Then, pin each colored-paper pattern piece to a piece of felt of the corresponding color. Cut out all the pieces and lay them on the whole pattern. Trim as necessary so the pieces fit together snugly. Then, use quick-grab, washable fabric glue to secure each piece to the coaster base. If desired, finish the edges using an overhand stitch and undivided embroidery floss. Hide the knots in between the layers of felt and secure with a dab of glue.

SHORTCUT/VARIATION:
Try using a rotary cutter, clear acrylic ruler, and a self-healing cutting mat to cut out the pieces more quickly and precisely. Use a tiny bit of glue from a basting glue stick to hold the paper pattern in place while cutting. Look at quilting books for other designs that can be translated to felt.

This woven trivet is made by simply coiling and securing fabric braids. Inexpensive, stretchy jersey is the best fabric to work with, because it can be easily formed into a variety of shapes and can be cleaned readily. Only about $^1/_8$ to $^1/_4$ of a yard (11 cm to 23 cm) of each color is necessary, so recycle those scraps or purchase discounted remainders from the fabric store. Try making a heart-shaped, oval, or square trivet, and experiment with different color patterns.

braided-rag trivet

starting out:

Cut the strips along the longest length of the fabric, if possible. The bigger the trivet gets, the longer the braids need to be to wrap completely around it.

1 **Wash, dry, and cut the jersey strips.** Using scissors, cut all the strips about 1 1/2" (4 cm) wide. The strips can be any size, but make sure they are all approximately the same, so that the trivet will be level. Larger strips will make fatter braids. Also, the strips don't need to be perfectly straight or have neat edges. Once braided, none of these imperfections will show.

2 **Make the braids.** Knot three strips of jersey together then tape the knot to a work surface. Next, weave the strips together to make a braid, the same way a hair braid is made. To do this, fan the strips out. Take the right-hand strip and fold it over the middle strip, then slide the middle strip to the far right. Next, take the left-hand strip and fold it over the new middle strip, bringing the middle strip to the far left. Repeat the procedure, alternating between left and right, until the strips are completely braided. Knot the ends to finish them.

3 **Form the trivet.** The sides of the braids will be the top and bottom of the trivet. Begin with the end of one braid, and point it down. Add a dab of glue to one of the wider sides of the braid at the end and begin coiling it. Add thin lines of glue in 3" (8 cm) sections, and continue coiling the braid. When finishing or starting a braid, cut the ends off at an angle so that they blend into the design, and secure them with glue to keep them from unraveling. Continue adding braids until the trivet reaches the desired size.

SHORTCUTS/VARIATIONS:
A smaller version of the trivet would make a great coaster, and a larger version could be used as a place mat. Try making a multicolored trivet reminiscent of a traditional rag rug by combining more than one color in each braid.

MATERIALS
• jersey, in assorted colors
• quick-grab, washable fabric glue
• sharp scissors
• masking tape

QUICK TIPS
Try using outgrown T-shirts to make the braids.

If continuing with a braid of the same color, match the ends up. If continuing with a different color, start it away from the end of the previous braid and coil it tightly around.

Use easy-cut steel to make the accents for this frame. The appliqués can be intricate or simple, as the ones here are. For more intricate designs, use a sharp craft knife rather than using scissors and replace the blade often. The design of these appliqués was inspired by antique hinges. Look at the hardware on old trunks and boxes at flea markets and yard sales for other pattern ideas.

metalwork
appliqué frame

MATERIALS

- unfinished wooden frame
- quick-rust ultra-thin steel
- apple cider vinegar
- white oil-based wood stain
- quick-grab adhesive
- spray acrylic sealer or varnish
- sponge brush
- fine sandpaper

starting out:

If quick-rust steel isn't available, use a rust finishing kit on any craft metal that's easy to cut, such as tin.

1 **Stain the frame.** First, sand the frame, if necessary, to smooth away any splinters or rough spots. Then, use a lint-free rag to apply white stain. Rub the stain with the grain of the wood, and wipe away or add more to achieve a transparent, white finish. Let the frame dry in a well-ventilated, low humidity area while preparing the appliqués.

2 **Cut and rust the metal appliqués.** Copy and cut out the pattern on page 99 and trace it on the metal sheet using a fine-point permanent marker. Then, cut out the appliqués with a pair of old scissors. Don't worry if the metal gets bent. Once it is rusted and glued to the frame, it will look fine. Next, follow the manufacturer's instructions for rusting. Submerge the steel for twenty to thirty minutes in apple cider vinegar. Use only a metal, non coated container. Touch the appliqués only on the edges and lean them up to dry. The rust will begin to appear as they dry. Be careful, because it can be smeared off easily at this point. Once they are dry, repeat the process if more rust is desired. Finally, let them dry, then spray a coat of sealer or varnish on them so they can be handled without smearing the rust.

3 **Apply the appliqués.** Use a lint-free rag to wipe any excess stain from the frame, especially where the metal accents will be applied. Then, use quick-grab glue to adhere the appliqués. Squeeze a thin line of glue all around the appliqués, close to the edges, so that it doesn't seep out from underneath. Press the appliqués into place for about 1 minute. If glue does seep out, gently wipe it away once it is dry. Dried quick-grab glues will often roll up into a ball if rubbed repeatedly, making it easier to remove. Finally, spray the entire frame with a coat of sealer or varnish.

SHORTCUTS/VARIATIONS:
Use real antique hinges as the accents for the frame, or buy new, interesting hinges and apply a rust finish. Also try using a shadow box frame and apply the accents along the sides to make it look like an old trunk. Then place an antique family treasure in it.

Clocks are a cinch to make, and with the variety of clip art available, personalizing one has never been easier. The old-fashioned art supplies used to mark the hour marks on this clock are copyright-free illustrations originally used for advertising. Clock-making kits are best, because they include all the necessary hardware, including nuts and washers, and will have an assembly diagram on the package. See Resources on page 104 for information on where to purchase clock-making kits.

craft-time
clock

MATERIALS
- unfinished wooden clock kit
- acrylic paint
- spray adhesive
- spray acrylic sealer or varnish
- sponge brush
- liner brush
- fine sandpaper

QUICK TIPS
To easily determine the placement of the images, trace the clock face on a piece of paper. Then, divide the circle into twelve equal-sized pie pieces. Center the pattern over the clock face, and poke a hole with a pencil through the paper at each line, about 1/2" (1 cm) in from the edge.

Use a permanent paint marker on the clock hands to color them any shade.

starting out:
The images used for this project are from *Scan This Book Two*, compiled by John Mendenhall. See Resources on page 104 for more information.

1 **Paint the clock face.** First, lightly sand the clock, if necessary, making sure to rid the surface of all particles. Next, paint the clock using a sponge brush for a minimum of brush strokes. The clock here has a beveled edge, which is painted a darker color. Use a line brush to accent fine grooves or ridges in the bevel with a third color.

2 **Photocopy and cut out the images.** First, decide what size the images need to be. Experiment with different sizes using a black-and-white photocopier. Photocopy the final art in color or black and white, on thin, matte, high-quality paper. Then, cut out the images as close to the edge as possible, using a craft knife for more intricate pictures.

3 **Decoupage the images to the clock face.** Use spray adhesive to decoupage the images to the clock. Since it doesn't soak the paper, it won't cause the colors to bleed or run. Press the images carefully but firmly in place. Then, spray a coat of sealer or varnish on the clock. Assemble the movement and hands according to the package directions.

SHORTCUT/VARIATION:
Many clip art books are printed on one side of the page, so the images can be cut directly from the book. Use a book with smaller "spot" art, so that the images can easily fit on the clock face.

weekend crafts

The projects in this section can be completed at a leisurely pace over a weekend. Many can be easily broken up into a few short sessions. Don't be intimidated because they seem more intricate. They are just as easy to make as any other project in this book. All the techniques and skills you need can be mastered with very little, if any, practice.

Larger projects may at first seem overwhelming. Avoid disappointment by being realistic about the time needed to complete the project—always assume it will take longer than expected. Then, take the project step by step, and allow enough time in one sitting to make some progress, so that the process is fulfilling rather than frustrating. One or two hours should be plenty. Finally, enlist the help of children and friends to make the time more enjoyable, as well as quicker.

Quick Tip: Spending more time on a project also allows for more personal expression and will get the creative juices flowing. Don't be afraid to experiment midstream or to change the project completely if the mood strikes. Ideally, the instructions in this section will serve as technical guidelines that can be easily adjusted to fit any decor or personal preference.

This paper valance is accented with carved shell beadwork and beaded fringe. The valance can be scaled to fit any window and can either be nailed into the window frame or set on hooks. Brightly colored paper will often visibly fade when exposed to direct sunlight, so take this into account when choosing materials. With lighter or pastel papers, fading won't be as obvious.

beaded paper
valance

starting out:

Use durable, handmade paper with lots of fabriclike texture for this project. The paper used to make this valance is similar to crinkled cotton.

MATERIALS

- tear-resistant, handmade paper in two colors
- beads
- embroidery floss
- dowel
- acrylic paint
- quick-grab adhesive
- large needle
- paintbrush
- scissors

1 **Cut the paper.** Measure the width of the window, and decide how far down the valance should hang. Cut a piece of paper to this size; this will be the valance base. Then, cut a top accent strip for the valance from the other paper. The accent strip should be twice the height desired, because it will fold over the dowel. Cut a lower accent strip, and lay it over the valance base so that the edges align. Glue the lower accent strip to the base, but leave the bottom half unattached so that the fringe threads can be embedded between the two papers.

2 **Cut the bottom edge of the valance.** Enlarge the pattern on page 102 to the needed size. The pattern will need to be copied in several pieces, then taped together. Cut out the pattern and tape it into place along the back bottom edge of the valance. Trace the pattern outline with a pencil, then cut the paper valance along the line.

3 **Attach the dowel for hanging.** First, paint the dowel. Adhere the dowel to the middle of the top accent strip using quick-grab adhesive. Then, fold the paper over the dowel and glue the flaps snugly to the top of the valance.

4 **Bead the top of the valance.** Use one or two strands of embroidery floss and a large needle to sew on the line of beads near the top. Bring the thread up through the paper, through the bead, and back through the paper near the original point of entry. Continue across. Once the beading is complete, secure the thread with a knot and a dab of glue.

5 **Make the fringe.** Select beads for the fringe that are long but have the hole close to one end. This way, they will dangle. For tubular beads, thread down the tube, through a smaller bead, then back through the tube. Mark equally spaced increments on the back of the valance and sew the beads at the marked points. Glue the front accent paper down to conceal the stitching.

Embroidery adds a comforting, homespun appeal to linens. The open, airy pattern on these pillowcases captures that feeling with a minimum of effort. One stitch, one thread, and a simple pattern make this project a great introduction to the needle arts.

easy embroidered bed linens

starting out:

Multicolored embroidery floss was used on these pillowcases to get a range of hues—from dark to light to dark again—without ever having to change the thread.

MATERIALS

- pillowcases or other linens
- embroidery floss
- embroidery needle
- dressmaker's transfer paper

1 **Mark the pattern.** Wash the pillowcases and iron the edges. Then, use dressmaker's transfer paper to mark the pattern on the pillowcase edges. To do this, first tape the pillowcase to a flat, hard work surface. Photocopy a pattern from page 103, slip transfer paper behind it, and secure both papers to the case with tape. Next, trace over the pattern lines with a ballpoint pen. Remove the pattern.

2 **Stitch the pattern.** Cut an arm's length of embroidery floss, knot one end, and thread the other end through the needle. Beginning at the point of the bottom diamond, or at one end of the curving line, push the needle up through the fabric from the back. Follow the pattern lines, sewing running stitches approximately $1/4$" (6 mm) long. To sew a running stitch, simply take the needle up through the fabric, then down, then up again, etc. Try to keep the stitches about the same length and distance from each other. Finish with a snug knot on the inside.

3 **Wash the pillowcases.** Apply a small dab of permanent fabric glue to the beginning and end knots to secure. Then, wash the to get rid of the transfer lines. Hand washing is not necessary.

 SHORTCUTS/VARIATIONS:
To make a quicker design, try stitching a couple of small stars or other simple outlined images. Also, try stitching a sheet to make a matching set.

QUICK TIPS

On the pillowcases here, a long-short-long sequence of stitching is used to make the line appear more solid. To do this, take the needle up through the fabric, then down again about a $1/4$" (6 mm) away; then, take the needle up through the fabric about $1/8$" (3 mm) away from the previous stitch.

Undivided, six-strand embroidery floss was used for these pillowcases. Divide the strands and use three or four to get a finer line.

At the end of a line, or at the turning point in a pattern, the length of the stitch may need to be shortened to follow the pattern. Make the last several stitches a tiny bit shorter, so that they still appear to be uniform.

This tray is decorated with squares of stained veneer edging, which is used to repair and finish cabinet edges and other pieces of furniture. It often has a layer of adhesive on the back, so that it can be easily ironed into position. Use it to make this project a little easier—and much less messy. It can be found at hardware and woodworking stores.

checker-board
iron-on veneer tray

MATERIALS

- iron-on veneer edging
- unfinished wooden serving tray
- thin cotton towel
- oil-based wood stain in blue, green, and white
- spray acrylic varnish
- craft knife
- iron
- fine sandpaper
- latex gloves

QUICK TIP

For added detail, position the grain of all the blue squares horizontally and the green squares vertically.

starting out:

Play with color. Oil-based wood stains can be intermixed for a range of hues.

1 **Determine the number of squares.** First, measure the interior tray bottom to determine how many squares will fit. Sketching it out on graph paper is helpful. The edging used here is $3/8$" (1 cm) wide, so, for simplicity, each square is $3/8$" (1 cm) to avoid making additional cuts. If the pattern doesn't work perfectly, try adding a border to fill out the space. Cut enough edging to cover the tray, but don't cut it into squares yet.

2 **Stain the veneer edging.** Use a lint-free rag, such as an old T-shirt, to apply the stain to the veneer strips. Rub on the stain in the direction of the wood grain. Wear latex gloves to avoid staining your hands. Use two colors for a checkerboard effect. Wipe the stain until the desired translucency is achieved, or add more to deepen the color. Let the strips dry for twenty-four hours.

3 **Stain the tray.** Lightly sand the tray, if necessary. Remove all dust and particles. Apply a coat of white stain to the edges and sides of the tray. Let dry for twenty-four hours.

4 **Cut and apply the squares.** Use a sharp craft knife to score the edging strips, then cut off the squares with scissors. Position all of the squares on the tray, making adjustments as necessary. Cover the veneer with the cotton cloth, then heat one small section at a time pressing down firmly with the iron (it should be on the cotton setting). Remove the iron after about fifteen seconds, and press the squares down with your hands or a small, round jar. The squares can always be reheated with the iron and shifted if necessary.

5 **Seal the tray.** Once the tray is cool, spray it with a coat of varnish, being sure to cover the sides and edges of the tray as well. Let the first coat dry completely, then apply another.

This picnic cloth is perfect for a lakeside lunch or a day at the beach. Start with a ready-made tablecloth, and personalize it with ribbon accents. Add a pocket to carry utensils, paperback books, sunscreen, or other conveniences. This cloth has ribbon closures, making it easy to transport. Just fold the cloth in half, roll it towards the ribbon closures, and tie.

portable
picnic cloth

MATERIALS

- tablecloth, washed and pressed
- 18" (46 cm) of fabric for the pocket, washed and pressed
- spools of ribbon in various sizes
- quick-grab washable fabric glue
- washable fabric marking pen
- paper-backed fusing tape
- iron

QUICK TIPS

Prevent the glue from bleeding through the ribbon by using a thin, even layer. Apply the ribbon in 3" (8 cm) sections so that the glue doesn't dry before the ribbon can be placed.

Use a pressing cloth when ironing the fusing tape to protect the surface of the iron.

1 **Apply the ribbons.** Cut the ribbon so that each variety measures 2" (5 cm) longer than the table-cloth width. Fold the ends over 1/8" (3 mm) for a clean edge, and use a small dab of permanent, washable glue to secure them. Then, use a ruler and a washable fabric marking pen to make a straight guideline across the cloth for the ribbon. Apply the ribbon with fusing tape or with washable fabric glue if the fusing tape is too wide for the ribbon. Wrap the extra inch (3 cm) of ribbon at each end around the cloth, and secure on the back with washable glue.

2 **Make the pocket.** Determine the size of the pocket needed by measuring what will go in it. Then, add 1" (3 cm) to the width and 1" (3 cm) to the height for finishing the edges. Cut the fabric using a rotary cutter, clear acrylic ruler, and cutting mat. Alternatively, mark the fabric with the washable pen and cut carefully with scissors. Next, iron fusing tape around all the edges on the back of the fabric. Fold both short edges by 1/2" (1 cm) over the adhesive, and iron in place. Do the same for the long edges, and secure the overlapping corners with washable glue.

3 **Apply the pocket.** Apply more fusing tape to the back of the pocket along the two short edges and one long edge. The other long side will be the pocket's opening. Add strips of fusing tape vertically along the pocket to divide it into sections. Then, pin the pocket in place on the cloth avoiding the areas with fusing tape. Finally, fuse the pocket to the cloth.

4 **Attach the ribbon closures.** Fold the short edges of the cloth in half with the back exposed. At one short edge, measure the center mark between the fold and the nearest corner. Mark with a washable pen. This will create two equal sections on either side of the mark. Then, mark the center of both those sections. This is where the ribbon ties will be attached. Cut two equal lengths of ribbon approximately 24" (61 cm) long, and finish the ends as described in step 2. Finally, fold the ribbons in half, and glue each at their halfway points to the marked spots on the cloth. Glue about 1/2" (1 cm) of the ribbons to the cloth.

 SHORTCUT/VARIATION:
Attach triangular pockets to the back of each corner on the cloth, then slip small rocks in each to prevent the cloth from fluttering on a breezy day.

The base of the handbag is cut from a piece of durable canvas, then beautified with delicate, embroidered eyelet fabric. No sewing is involved, and the pattern can be scaled to any size, from handbag to tote bag. For larger bags, be sure to choose a strong material for the handles and use plenty of adhesive.

no-sew
handbag

starting out:

Grosgrain ribbon was used for this bag because of its strength and ability to hold its shape. Only use sheer ribbons for small bags that won't be loaded with heavy objects.

MATERIALS
- 1 yard (91 cm) of canvas
- 1 yard (91 cm) of eyelet fabric
- wide, durable ribbon for the handle
- ribbon to trim the edges
- quick-grab washable fabric glue
- washable fabric marking pen
- paper-backed fusing tape
- iron

1 **Cut the canvas base.** Copy the pattern on page 103 to any size. Then, pin it to a piece of washed, pressed canvas. Trace the pattern with a washable fabric marking pen. Next, use a rotary cutter, cutting mat, and a clear acrylic ruler to cut the fabric according to the pattern.

2 **Cut the eyelet fabric.** Cut five individual pieces of eyelet to cover the sides, bottom, front, and back of the canvas purse. The eyelet doesn't need to cover the flaps. The eyelet needs to be applied in segments in order to lie smoothly over the canvas.

3 **Apply the eyelet to the canvas.** Iron fusing tape, paper side up, along the edges of each eyelet piece. Then, position the eyelet pieces on the canvas and iron smoothly into place. Use a pressing cloth over the eyelet to protect the iron from the adhesive.

4 **Put the bag together.** Apply quick-grab washable fabric glue to the flaps on the same side of the canvas as the eyelet. Fold the bag sides up to meet the flaps, and secure the flaps on the side without the eyelet.

5 **Add the ribbon trim and handle.** Use sharp scissors to cut twelve pieces of ribbon, one for each edge of the bag. Cut the ribbon to fit each edge perfectly. Then, fold the ribbons down the middle, lengthwise, and squeeze a line of quick-grab glue along the crease. Apply the ribbons to the edges of the bag, then glue them down completely. Finally, cut two equal lengths of ribbon for the handle, and glue them to the inside of the bag. Make sure they are aligned with each other before securing them.

QUICK TIP
Press a crease along the bag's fold lines before putting the bag together to give it a more defined shape.

SHORTCUT/VARIATION:
Use patterned canvas and skip the eyelet altogether. Draw a fabric marker design, iron on appliqués, or glue fabric flowers to the bag for quick details. Also try adding a Velcro closure to the bag.

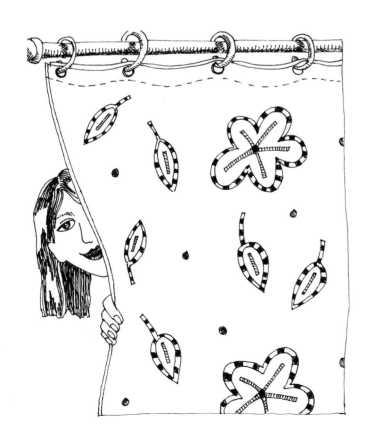

a gallery of
quick crafts

The following pages contain twenty quick ideas from Jane Asper that are as fun to look at as they are easy to make. Try photocopying and cutting them out to start a crafty recipe box. Mount them on index cards. Then add photos, color swatches, quick sketches, and any other inspiring images from magazines, books, newspapers, or catalogs. This is sure to build a handy reference that will spark ideas when planning future projects or designs.

Jane Asper is a Denver-based craft designer and writer whose work appears weekly in the *Rocky Mountain News*.

Places, Everyone!

Buy clear vinyl at the fabric store. Cut 2 pieces, 11"x 17". Lay your child's artwork, your husband's favorite comic strips, pictures cut from magazines, family snapshots, etc., on one sheet. Cover w/ 2nd sheet. Punch holes all round, lace together with ribbon or yarn. Make 1 for everyone!

Shower Power

Use permanent Magic Markers to draw or trace on a clear plastic shower curtain. Use over a colored plastic liner. For best results, stick to simple line drawings.

...and Pretty Plates All in a Row

You chipped a china saucer? Dinged a darling dish? That's the start of a fun edging for a flower bed. Simply imbed the flawed side ½ way into the soil & pack tightly, overlapping dishes as you go.

Easy Pillows

Purchase two 20" napkins, (either matching or coordinating) one 16" pillow form & embroidery floss. Put napkins together right sides out. Sew them together 2" from edge on 3 sides using floss. Insert pillow form, sew fourth side closed. Could it be any easier?

P. O. B. 101101 Denver, Co. 80250

Birthday Crown

For the base, rip apart a grapevine wreath from the craft store. Use florist wire to re-wire pieces into head-sized crown. Pick lots of leaves & flowers, wire into bundles. Then wire bundles on to crown. Add ribbons to tie under chin.

Petal Pushers

Use wire cutters to cut stems off "silk" flowers. Use E 6000 glue to attach layers of petals together. When dry, push pin through petal group & glue to base of push pin head. Or if you want, glue a bead on top & a magnet on the back.

Take time to smell the flowers

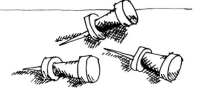

Sachet Pouf

Use a saucer to trace a circle on the wrong side of any soft cotton fabric. Cut out. 1. Hand sew a running stitch all around the edge. 2. Pull ½ way closed. Fill w/ lavender. 3. Pull thread tight, knot. Add small circle of fabric, button, sew button through bottom of pouf. Knot, cut thread.

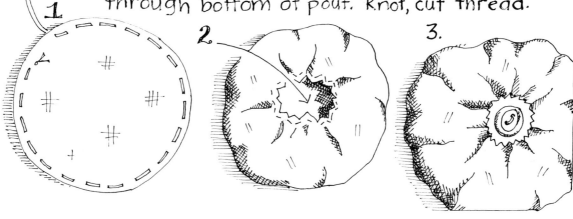

Finger Puppets

Cut the fingers off a pair of colored knit gloves. Whip stitch the bottom edges to prevent ravelling. Use bits of felt, yarn & beads to make animal faces and tails on each one.

BEFORE

AFTER

Bed Time Story Pillow Case

Slide a large piece of cardboard inside a pillow case. Then use a fabric marker to write the first few lines of your child's favorite story on the pillow case. Remove cardboard, insert pillow, sleep tight, don't let the bed bugs bite.

Switch Your Plates

Buy plain, dull plastic switchplates and turn them into something fun. Paint them with acrylics, if you wish. Or use clear acrylic medium to affix and coat collage materials. Or cover with a page from a book. Or use wrapping or wall paper. Or?...

P.O.B. 101101 DENVER, COLO. 80250

Harvest Compote

Use a large clay plant saucer for the bowl and an inverted small pot for the stand. Glue together w/2 part epoxy glue. Leave as is or paint and/or decorate any way you choose.

Book Shelf

Use any pretty book that isn't a valuable antique to make this project. Purchase 2 simple shelf supports and use screws to attach them to the bottom of the book. Attach to wall following shelf support instructions.

LITTLE WOME

Chair Pocket

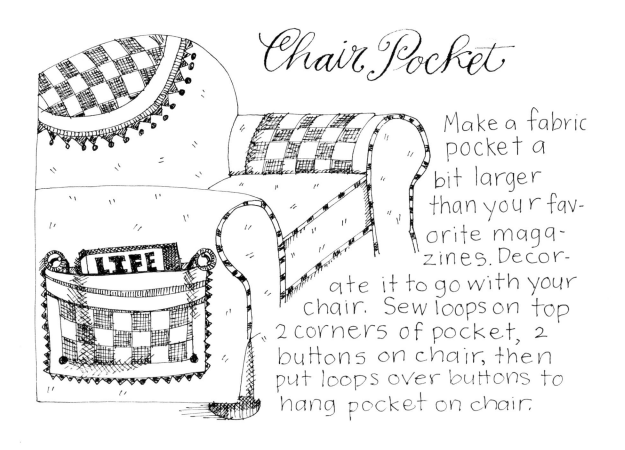

Make a fabric pocket a bit larger than your favorite magazines. Decorate it to go with your chair. Sew loops on top 2 corners of pocket, 2 buttons on chair, then put loops over buttons to hang pocket on chair.

A Real Corker

Let's hope you saved all the corks from your holiday libations! Glue them flat in a shallow box lid.

Cover edge w/ glued on ribbon. Add a hanger on the back, hang up in the kitchen for a great looking bulletin board. Cheers!

Remember to pick up wine

Woven Throw

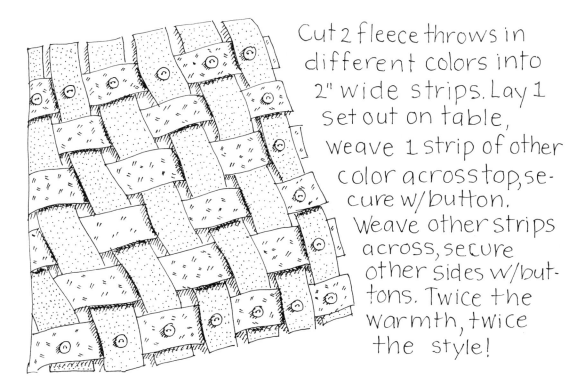

Cut 2 fleece throws in different colors into 2" wide strips. Lay 1 set out on table, weave 1 strip of other color across top, secure w/button. Weave other strips across, secure other sides w/buttons. Twice the warmth, twice the style!

Mosaic Stepping Stones

Buy inexpensive concrete stepping stones and a bag of ceramic tile mortar at the home center. Use a hammer to break ceramic tiles and/or old pretty plates into flat small pieces. Mix mortar according to directions, apply to dampened stepping stones. Press tiles, etc. into mortar. Smooth edge w/a ruler. After mortar starts to set, brush off excess mortar on top w/a damp rag. Cure for 24 hours before using.

P.O.B. 101101 Denver, Co. 80250

Sunflowers & Morning Glories

Buy a packet each of sunflower and morning glory seeds. Nick the m.g. seeds w/a utility knife, soak in water overnight. In a pot or the ground, plant a sunflower seed in the center and a ring of m.g.'s around it. The sunflower is strong enough to support the morning glories, & both grow at the same rate— REALLY FAST!

P.O.B. 101101 Denver, Co. 80250

Hob Knob

Instead of regular knobs on a chest or cupboard, try these ideas instead:

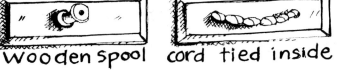

Wooden spool   cord tied inside   ribbon tied outside

Conversely, use regular knobs for other purposes.

Old door knobs make great coat hooks

Hang pictures from dresser knobs

Use handles for tie backs

Occasional Candles

Inexpensive glass-clad holy candles are available at many grocery and discount stores. They come in all different colors. For this project, you'll want one without a label. Use self-stick label paper, markers and your imagination to turn these candles into festive, personalized presents.

★ Happy
30th Birth
★ Vanessa

P.S. If you th
You feel old,
what about
me? Love, Mom.

P.O.B. 101101 Denver, Colo. 80250

Gold Mesh Votive Holder

Buy some brass window screen (a.k.a "gold mesh") from the hardware store. Wear work gloves to cut a 12"x12" square. Center plain glass votive holder on mesh, then gather mesh up around holder & secure with thin wire. Open out corners, arrange. Insert candle & light. Wa-la!

P O B 101101 Denver Co 80250

how to use quick craft
patterns

To use a pattern in this book, start by determining the size it needs to be. The easiest way to do this is by photocopying the template and experimenting with reducing or enlarging the image to discover the size that works best.

Depending on the project, the pattern can be made from paper; adhesive vinyl; or thin, flexible cardboard. If a pattern will be used often, make it out of cardboard so it can be reused several times. To transfer the properly sized, photocopied pattern to a piece of cardboard, simply cut it out and trace it. Then use a craft knife or scissors to cut the cardboard. For transferring a pattern to very curved surfaces, such as a round vase or cup, adhesive vinyl is a better choice. It also works well on glass, wood, or metal surfaces. To transfer a pattern to a piece of adhesive vinyl, cut out the pattern and trace it using a permanent marker.

Quick Tip: For a quicker alternative to cutting out and tracing a pattern, use graphite transfer paper. It is also ideal when working with more complex patterns with interior lines. Graphite transfer paper is available at art and craft supply stores. To use it, place a piece under a photocopied pattern and draw over the lines. This works best with wood or paper projects.

Layered Window Cards

(page 23)

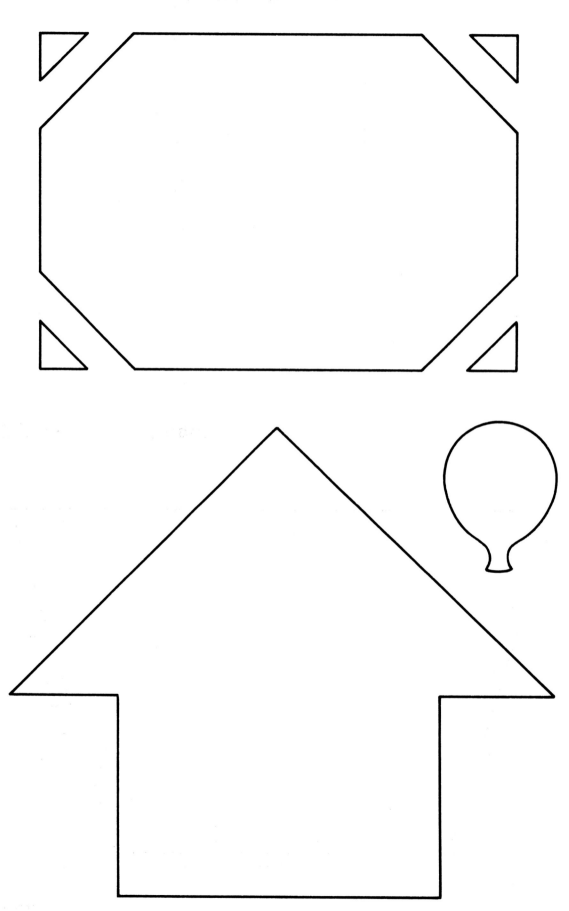

Laced Letter Holder

(page 41)

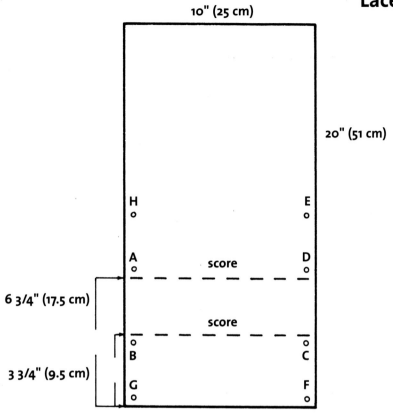

10" (25 cm)

20" (51 cm)

H
E
A
score
D
6 3/4" (17.5 cm)
score
B
C
3 3/4" (9.5 cm)
G
F

Embossed Paper Bowl & Tray

(page 43)

(enlarge pattern)

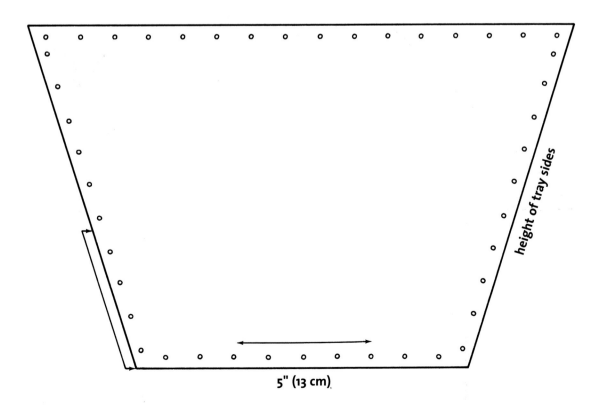

height of tray sides

5" (13 cm)

Cut-Paper Window Shade

(page 45)

Hand-Illustrated Cocktail Napkins

(page 51)

Crumpled-Copper Candle Shades

(page 53)

Cut out tone areas

Flowerpot Trellis

(page 61)

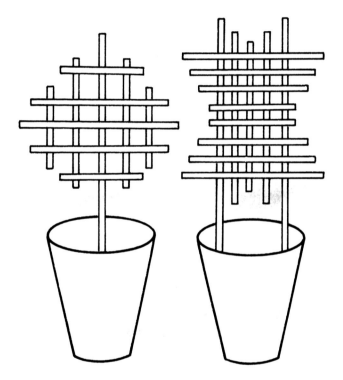

Metalwork Appliqué Frame

(page 67)

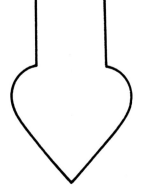

Quilt-Inspired Felt Coasters

(page 63)

Star

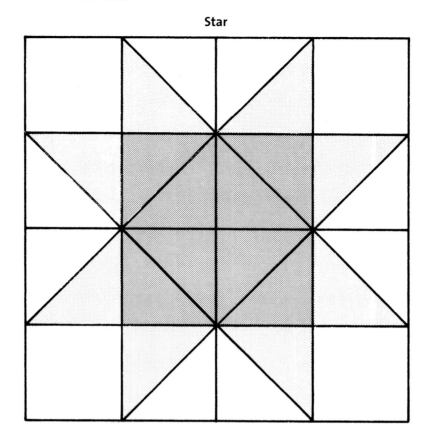

Rail Fence

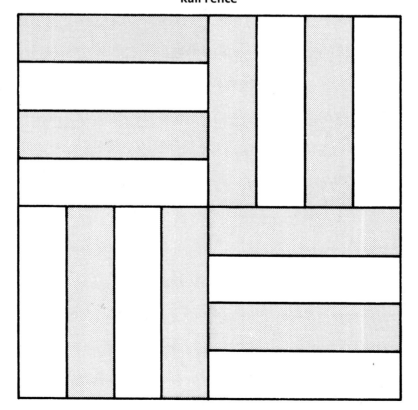

Oh Susannah

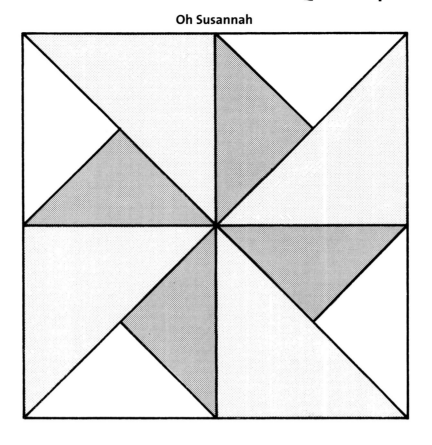

Crazy Quilt

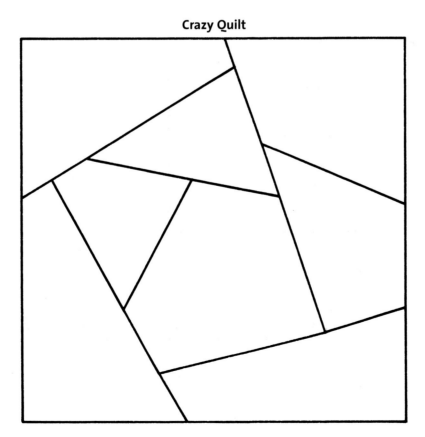

Beaded Paper Valance

(page 73)

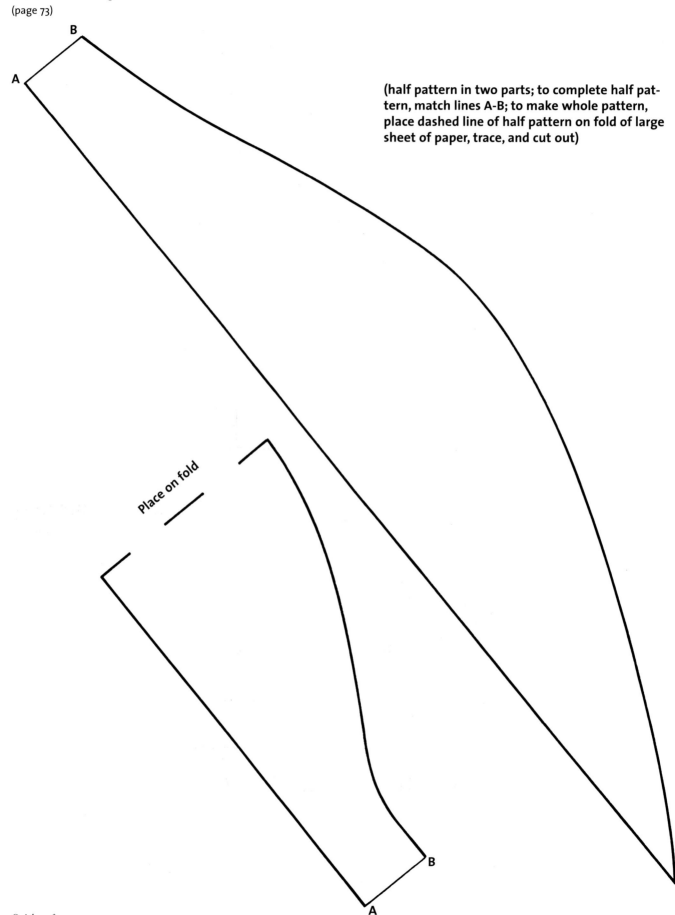

(half pattern in two parts; to complete half pattern, match lines A-B; to make whole pattern, place dashed line of half pattern on fold of large sheet of paper, trace, and cut out)

Place on fold

Easy Embroidered Bed Linens

(page 75)

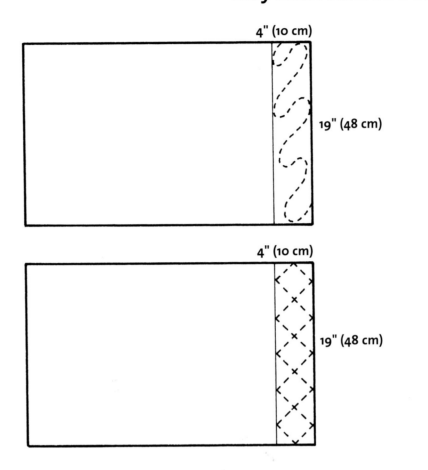

4" (10 cm)

19" (48 cm)

4" (10 cm)

19" (48 cm)

No-Sew Handbag

(page 81)

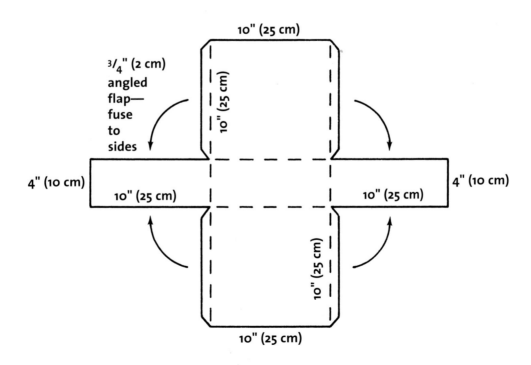

10" (25 cm)

³/₄" (2 cm) angled flap— fuse to sides

10" (25 cm)

4" (10 cm)

10" (25 cm)

10" (25 cm)

4" (10 cm)

10" (25 cm)

10" (25 cm)

resources

The following mail-order resources offer a variety of standard and unique craft supplies, including some of the harder-to-find materials used in this book.

American Art Clay Co., Inc. (AMACO)
4717 W. 16th Street
Indianapolis, IN 46222 USA
phone: 800-374-1600
email: catalog@amaco.com
web site: http://www.amaco.com

European Office:
PO Box 467
Longton, Stoke-On-Trent
ST3 7DN, UK
phone: 01782 399219
email: andrewcarter@amaco.uk.co

AMACO manufactures and sells wire mesh, embossing foils, and Rub-N-Buff gilding creams, as well as other craft supplies and numerous pottery-related products.

Art Direction Book Co., Inc.
456 Glenbrook Road
Glenbrook, CT 06906
phone: 203-353-1441

The Art Direction Book Co. publishes books on graphic design and the Scan This Book clip art book series.

The Art Store
4004 Hillsboro Pike
Nashville, TN 37215
phone: 800-999-4601
web site:
http://www.artstoreplus.com

The Art Store sells supplies for the professional and amateur, including brush pens, glass paints, rubber stamps, and bookbinding materials.

B & B Etching Products
18700 N. 107th Avenue #13
Sun City, AZ 85373-9759
phone: 623-933-4567
web site: http://www.etchall.com

B & B Etching Products manufactures and sells the etchall line of products used in several projects in this book. They offer several glass items, such as

jars and beveled ornaments. They will also create adhesive vinyl stencils from sketches for a small fee. This eliminates the need to cut out a complex design by hand.

Dover Publications
Customer Care Department
31 East 2nd Street
Mineola, NY 11501-3852
fax: 516-742-6953
web site:
http://store.doverpublications.com/

Dover Publications offers a staggering array of clip art books with themes ranging from cigar box labels to Japanese design motifs. Many books have been printed on only one side of the page, making it easy to cut and use the images for découpage. Request a free catalog of clip-art titles by going to the web site or writing to the above address.

Fire Mountain Gems
28195 Redwood Highway
Cave Junction, OR 97523-9304 USA
phone: 800-423-2319
email: questions@firemtn.com
web site: http://www.firemoun-taingems.com/

Fire Mountain Gems sells everything necessary for making jewelry, including semi-precious beads, handmade glass beads, silver and copper beads, wire, findings, and tools.

HobbyCraft
(stores nationwide)
Head Office
Bournemouth, United Kingdom
phone: 01202 596100

John Lewis
Head Office
Oxford Street
London W1A 1EX, United Kingdom
phone: 020 7269 7711

Loose Ends
PO Box 20310
Salem, OR 97307-0310
phone: 503-393-2348
email: info@looseends.com
web site: http://www.4loosends.com/

Loose Ends offers gorgeous and unusual handmade papers. They also sell a variety of natural items including raffia, bamboo, fabrics, papier-mâché forms, and tin ware.

Paper Clips
PO Box 492
Mendham, NJ 07945
email: PaperClips4U@aol.com

Paper Clips sells packet folios of vintage papers for crafting, including maps, book pages in several languages, sheet music, stamps, old photographs, and receipts. They will also customize packets for specific projects.

Pearl Paint
308 Canal Street
New York, New York 10013
phone: for Domestic Mail Order, 800-221-6845 x2297; for International Mail Order, 212-431-7932 x2297
web site: http://pearlpaint.com

Pearl Paint is a great resource for general art and craft supplies, including metal leaf in several colors, wood stains, spray adhesive, and tools.

Walnut Hollow Farm, Inc.
1409 State Road 23
Dodgeville, WI 53533
phone: 800-950-5101
web site:
http://www.walnuthollow.com/

Walnut Hollow offers unfinished wood items, including frames, shelves, trays, and boxes. They also sell everything necessary for clock making.

about the author

Livia McRee is a craft writer and designer who is always looking for the best, but short-est-way to make beautiful crafts. Born in Nashville and raised in New York City by her working-artist parents, Livia has always been captivated by and immersed in folk and fine arts, as well as graphic design. She now lives in California.

She is the author of *Instant Fabric: Quilted Projects from Your Home Computer*. She has also contributed to numerous other books, including *The Crafter's Project Book*, *The Stamp Artist's Project Book*, *The Right Light*, *Paper House*, *Simple Elegance*, and *Ceramic Painting Color Workshop*, all by Rockport Publishers.

Jane Asper lives in Denver, Colorado, where she is a craft designer and writer. She has been published in various books and magazines, and her work appears weekly in the *Rocky Mountain News*.

acknowledgments

Many talented people come together and add their own special touch to make a book like this.

First and foremost, I'd like to thank Mary Ann Hall, who keeps everything running smoothly and inspires me constantly; Maryellen Driscoll, my friend and copy editor, who is one of the most multi-talented and wonderful people I know; Jane Asper, for contributing her unique whimsical touch to this book; Barbara C. Bosler of B & B Etching Products, Inc., who is always so helpful; Shawna Mullen, a visionary editor who is such a delight to work with; Martha Wetherill, whose comforting demeanor and easygoing attitude are always appreciated; Jay Donahue, whose humor and behind-the-scenes skill make it all come together; Roberta Frauwirth, the talented pattern illustrator; and everyone else at Rockport Publishers, especially the art directors, designers, and photographers, who do such beautiful work.

Special thanks to my mother Giorgetta McRee, who taught me how to meet impossible deadlines. (She has been known to put together a one-woman art show in a day.) And to my father Leo McRee, whose attention to detail during the artistic process is unrivaled. He inspires me to always do my best.

As always, all my love and gratitude to Biz Stone, who helps me in countless ways, day in and day out.